Fox and Dad

BEVERLY DETROY

authorHOUSE®

AuthorHouse™
1663 Liberty Drive
Bloomington, IN 47403
www.authorhouse.com
Phone: 833-262-8899

Published by AuthorHouse 09/20/2021

ISBN: 978-1-4685-7349-7 (sc)
ISBN: 978-1-4685-7348-0 (e)

CONTENTS

I. BEGINNING 1

II. FAMILY HISTORY 29

III. GANG.. 53

IV. GANG GOES FISHING...................................... 85

V. GANG AT PLAY... 111

VI. LAWRENCE AND BEVERLY IN ITALY.......................... 131

VII. BUSINESS 143

VIII. KIDS... 173

IX. PETS 195

X. GOOD-BYES 211

I. BEGINNING

Busgirl
The Sweater
Lawrence
True Commitment
Background: Irish and Lebanese

BUSGIRL

I got a job at Stouffer's as a busgirl. I was 16 and I came from a really protective family. My mother was really strict. There were eight children; I was the oldest daughter, and they would not let me go anywhere or do anything. I was allowed to join one club a year. I was allowed to go out on a date one night a week, and my mother grounded me three weekends out of the month, for crazy reasons, but that's the way people did it.

The only job I had ever done was babysit. So I told her, "I'm going to get a job."

She said, "If you can get a job, okay. I'll accept it."

The bus picked me up outside of my house at Standiford Lane, and I had never gone anywhere. Literally, totally, totally sheltered — never went anywhere. So I asked the bus driver, "Where does this bus go?"

He said, "Well, it's going to go downtown."

"Okay. Downtown sounds like a good place to get a job."

So I get on the bus and I'm sitting up front. You've got to imagine, I'm wearing my hair in a ponytail. I told the busdriver, "I don't want to get lost. I don't know where I'm at, but I'll tell you when I want to get off."

He says, "Just sit up here by me."

So we go driving downtown, and you've got all these stops and gos, stops and gos. And I see this line of people out on the street on Broadway, at the corner of Second and Broadway, and I said, "What's that?"

And he said, "Oh, that's a new place that's open. It's called Stouffer's. Everybody in town wants to get a job there."

I said, "Well, who are all those people there?"

"Well, they're in line to get a job."

I said, "Well, okay. Let me out here." I asked, "Do you pick me up here? Can I get straight to my house from this spot?"

"Oh yeah, this bus goes straight from here to your house."

So I thought, "Well, that's perfect," because I had no transportation.

So I get out, and I'm 16. And I obviously look 16, believe me. I get in line, and they tell me they're not hiring anybody unless they're 21. I said, "Well, that's okay." I wanted a job.

Then these people come through and they hand out applications. They said, "Are you 21?"

I said, "No."

The man said, "You can't interview."

I said, "That's okay. I'm standing in line."

He said, "You don't understand. We don't hire anyone underage." Stouffer's food company was a family-owned operation, and they were very careful about serving liquor. They did not want to serve liquor, but when they did have places that served liquor, they were very careful about making sure that everybody was 21 and all the other details.

But I wanted a job and I was determined, and my mother told me that if I didn't get a job that day, then I'd have to continue on with babysitting, so I was bound and determined. I'm standing in line and they keep passing me up and they won't give me an application. And everybody's glaring at me and telling me, "You know you can't be here. You're supposed to leave. You have to be 21." "You know this," and "you know that." I ignore them.

So I get all the way in, now the line was all the way out past the Portland Federal building. It went into the Stouffer's building, inside and down in the basement to their employment office.

So I get all the way in. This takes hours. They're hollering at me to get out of line, and I ignore them. So then finally there was this lady, her name was Miss Kozack and I really liked this lady. She was so mean, she was so evil, and I loved her. She was like real strict; she reminded me of a matron in a penitentiary. I mean, if you ever knew a matron in a penitentiary, this would be the perfect person. Coal black hair, black horn-rimmed glasses, tie-up shoes. They wore those tie-up shoes with the big, thick heels. That's Miss Kozack.

She said, "What are you doing here? Are you the kid that's been standing in line all day?"

"Yes, ma'am."

"What the hell do you think you're doing?"

"I'm applying for work."

"Don't you know we're only hiring people 21?"

"Yeah."

"Get out of the line!"

"Nope. Not 'til you interview me. Not till you give me an application."

So she said, "No. Just go home. Call your mother. Go!" But I wouldn't go.

I get all the way down the steps and they make me get out of line, and they set me on a settee. This little settee, and they said, "Sit!"

And she came out and she said, "Sit!" So I went over there and I sat.

She interviews everybody. It's getting dark. I know I'm in trouble because I've been gone all day long and my mother's going to kill me. I had to follow rules with my mother. I'm thinking, "Oh my God, I'm not going to get the job. My mother's never going to believe me."

Mrs. Kozack calls me in the office and says, "I want to know why you wouldn't get out of the line."

I said, "Because I know you have to have something for me to do."

"How old are you?"

"I'm 18."

"How old are you?"

"I'm 16. But I'll say I'm 18, so it'll get you through the papers."

"Okay. I'll make you a busgirl. But you can't pick up wine glasses. You can't pick up liquor glasses" and a dozen other rules.

"Okay. Fine." I got the job.

I was thrilled to death. I didn't know what I was getting paid. I didn't know what hours I was going to work. I was just thrilled I got a job.

I went home, and my mother wanted to kill me. It was dark when I got home, and she was furious. So I explained to her I got the job, and how great it was.

So I go to work at Stouffer's, and I'm a busgirl. I'm the only kid there. The other employees are "women," and they're "adults."

The place opens, and right away they've got a lot of business.

And there's always this little rumble through the dining room during lunchtime when this entourage arrives. I'm just a kid. I'm watching them. I'm thinking, "Who are those people?" And it was Frank Haddad and Lawrence Detroy and their "entourage" of people. When they went in there and sat down, they could have five or six men with them. They could have just them. It didn't matter. Everybody in the dining room vied for their attention. People would come over, they'd tell their story, they'd ask for advice, they would laugh. Everyone would come over to this table, and these two men would entertain or give advice or take them aside and speak in confidence. I'd just watch them. I'd think, "Well, this is pretty cool. I think that's pretty neat. I wonder who those two guys are."

Then I was their busgirl, and they really liked me. Lawrence liked me more than he should have. He followed me home, which today would be called stalking.

But I went on to college.

I'll always remember watching these guys. I thought, it's amazing how these men — the whole dining room could go quiet, and they'd walk in, and it would be, everything would come to life. I mean, it would be waitresses, it'd be busboys, it would be bellmen — everybody had a problem, everybody had a story to tell. They all wanted to discuss it with Lawrence and Frank.

The funniest thing was, when I was going to college, Lawrence and I never dated. He never was out of line with me. He was always a gentleman. I never even thought about him as anything other than Mr. Detroy. I didn't trust him. I was in awe of him, but I didn't let my guard down around him.

THE SWEATER

Lawrence Detroy and Frank Haddad were fascinating men.
I dearly loved Lawrence. I met him in 1964. I was sixteen-and-a-half years old, in my first real job, working as a busgirl at Stouffer's Food Corporation on Second and Broadway.

I was preparing to go to college, and the furthest thing from my mind was to meet anybody like Lawrence Detroy or Frank Haddad. I remember watching all of the different characters who came into Second and Broadway for lunch.

There were the ladies from the 800 that lived in the 800 Towers downtown. Two in particular that were something. I'd nickname everybody. One woman, I called her the "Afghan." She was tall and skinny and elegant. Real severe hairdo. And then a little short lady looked like a "Pekinese" — flou-flou. She wore frilly dresses, and a lot of flowers, and had her hair all curly and, as extreme and streamlined as the "Afghan" was, the "Pekinese" was the exact opposite.

These two women came in the dining room almost every day and commanded a lot of attention. There was the "Extenda-Care Gang" — a group of lawyers that came across the street from the Portland Federal Building every day for lunch and would sit at a table. Most of the servers did not want to wait on them because they did not tip. They would sit there, this group of men, and discuss an idea that they had, a concept, for a business they named Extenda-Care, which eventually turned into

Humana. There was Wendell Cherry, Carl Pollard, and David Jones, and several other men. Every day they'd come in the dining room.

Many, many business people, and secretaries, and a big variety of people, day in and day out, came into Stouffer's for lunch.

I had the privilege, as a busgirl, to work in and out of all these different tables and this variety of customers at Stouffer's, and, being a kid and being ever fascinated with people in general, I would eavesdrop and pick up on different stories and situations with all these individuals.

The thing I remember most vividly was when I first began to notice Lawrence Detroy and Frank Haddad entering the dining room every day. They would come in with a variety of businessmen. It would usually be maybe five or six of them. When they would come to the door, it was like everybody in the dining room focused on these two men, and I used to be amazed watching them. One was tall, and the other was short, but you could tell there was a kinship between these two men. They were always laughing and telling stories. The servers and the hostesses would hustle around and try to get them a prime location. There was generally a little maneuvering amongst the waitresses, because they all wanted to wait on these particular men. They were interesting and they tipped well!

When Frank and Lawrence would be seated finally, I would watch, one by one, different people go to them and ask advice, or tell their stories — or ask them to tell a story. And Lawrence and Frank would sit there, and hold court. But not in a manner that was egotistical. It was in a manner that showed they truly loved people.

Carl, the Room Service man, would come up. He had a lot of children and it seemed like he always had some sort of problem. He would ask advice. And, depending on what kind of advice he was asking, he would ask either Lawrence or Frank, or the two of them together would come up with some sort of solution to his problem.

There was a variety of businessmen who would come by and talk to these two guys. I didn't really know them, other than to remove glasses from the table or to get them more coffee, or whatever. But for several years I observed them. I was fascinated by them. But I was going to college, and my interests were in lots of other areas than Lawrence Detroy and Frank Haddad.

I think the first time I noticed Lawrence as a man was when I worked with a girl named Janie.

Janie and I would walk during the breaktime to Selman's downtown, or Byck's or Stewart's to window shop and look at all the different clothes. We both were the same age and we were both going to college. This particular year the main thing "in" was a cable-knit sweater, and Selman's had them. They were navy blue with gold buttons. Gosh, you just had to have these sweaters.

Neither one of us had money. So we both decided to put the sweaters on layaway, and so we would faithfully go to Selman's and put down a couple of dollars every day on these sweaters. The price was horrendous. It was $35 – $40, and it was like you'd never, ever achieve this amount of money. But we were determined to buy these sweaters.

We finally did, and she and I were so proud. We put them on, and they looked so cool. We knew we were the best-looking people in the world wearing these sweaters.

The day after we purchased the sweaters, I came into work, and Janie and I went to the top floor, which was the twelfth floor dining room, and we set up for lunch. We set out the ice and the butters and all the rest. I went to the dressing room, but my friend wasn't there. So I thought, "Well, she went on up ahead."

So I went up the elevator, and as the elevator was getting closer to the twelfth floor, I heard a strange noise, and when the elevator door opened, I saw it's my friend, and she was sitting on the leather bankette in the foyer outside the dining room just wailing and crying.

I asked her, "What in the world is wrong?" I thought something horrible had happened to her family or something. She was devastated and hysterical.

She said, "You won't believe what happened to me." She sobbed. "I went to the locker to unlock it where I'd left my sweater overnight. When I came in to get it, somebody had broken the locker and stolen my sweater." You might as well have taken this girl's heart out and stomped it in the ground, as to take this sweater that she and I had worked so hard to purchase on layaway. The sweater was everything — the world — to a teenage girl.

I tried to comfort my friend, and I got just as upset. I remember thinking, "How could anyone do that to us? How could anyone take her sweater?" The elevator door opened, and off the elevator stepped Lawrence Detroy. He came into the dining room early, I believe because he was going to try to arrange for a larger table he needed that day for lunch. Sometimes he would do that.

Anyway, Lawrence discovered my friend Janie and me sitting on the bench. Janie was crying hysterically, and he was quite concerned at what the problem was. So he asked.

Janie couldn't stop crying. She was just wailing, over and over again, and carrying on. I tried to verbalize to Mr. Detroy (as I called him at that time) what had happened. I explained to him about the sweater and that it was stolen, and how important this sweater was to Janie and why she was so very upset.

He stooped down and took my friend's hand, and calmly talked to her about the situation. And he actually got her to stop crying. He talked to her. He said, "The sweater is not that important. It's a bad thing that has happened to you, but the sweater is not important in the scheme of things." He comforted her and said things to her that helped her put in perspective the true situation.

Then she and I had to go to work. Janie did calm down, and through the rest of the shift we were able to get through the job. You had to put up a front and you had to pretend like everything was alright because you were dealing with the public. Our key function was to serve people.

Throughout that afternoon, I thought about this man who took his time to talk to my friend and myself, two teenagers that most people would ignore or say were silly. It stuck in my mind.

The next morning when we came to work, I met my friend in the locker room, and she was the exact opposite as she was the day before. As hysterical, upset, crying and wounded as she was the day before, she was now happy and gregarious and laughing and squealing, like she was cheering at a football game for the winning team.

"Now what, Janie?"

She said, "You won't believe this." She said, "I get to work this morning and they tell me there's a package here for me." And she had the box — a Selman's box. In the Selman's box is this sweater. It's a replacement sweater, but it is the sweater that she had bought.

My first instinct was, Mr. Detroy did this. There was no card. There was nothing that said where the sweater came from, only that the sweater was to be given to Janie. This package was to be given to Janie. I knew in my heart Mr. Detroy bought that sweater. I fronted him that day and asked him, and he said, "I don't know what you're talking about." He dummied up.

Over the years, as our relationship evolved, I periodically asked him about that sweater. He would never admit to purchasing it for my friend. But I know in my heart that he did. That was the kind of man he was. He didn't buy the sweater to fourflush. He didn't buy the sweater to impress anybody. He bought the sweater because he saw how very important this article of clothing was to a teenager. It may not have been. It didn't change anybody's life; it didn't change the world. But it was just an essential element in this girl's life, and he saw that. He picked up on it, and did something about it.

Lawrence

I think back to my childhood and my teenage years, and I realize what a truly happy time that was for me. I came from a large family of five boys and three girls. My mother and father were hardworking and strict.

Being the oldest daughter, I endured a lot of rules that were, as time went on with the other sisters, lightened up. My mother wisely protected me and prevented me from getting into trouble a lot of times, now that I look back and think about it. She permitted me to go out on a date one day a week, during my junior and senior year in high school, and then would come up with some excuse to ground me at least two weekends out of the month. My mother was able to control me and keep me home much of the time, or encouraged my friends to come to my house to keep me from going out.

As I went to college I had different boyfriends and fellows that I liked, and I continued to work at Stouffer's on the weekends. I frequently came home on the weekends to wait tables (as I got a little older, I was privileged to wait the tables) with a girlfriend, and we made a lot of money doing that. It was a great job. Although it took us five hours to drive to Louisville from Murray, and back again, we loved it. There's a lot to be said for the enthusiasm of youth. It's not a big deal to travel like that just to work a waitress job. But it wasn't just any waitress job. It was a job in a place that was truly fascinating and exciting to work.

I had a boyfriend that I really liked, and that my mother really liked. I thought I was in love. We were talking of marriage, and he was everything that any mother would probably want for her daughter. He was nice-looking, intelligent, a gentleman, thoroughly successful, appealing in most ways, and we were talking of marriage. I really thought I was going to marry this man. My mother just adored him. I remember I was at Stouffer's working, I was relieving a cashier one afternoon, and this man came to pick me up from work.

Frank Haddad and Lawrence Detroy had come to the register to settle up their bill, and my friend had come in to pick me up, and I was running late. I was relieving the cashier for a minute. I introduced my friend to Lawrence and Frank. I said, "Mr. Haddad, this is So-and-So. This is the gentleman I'm going to marry." And Frank was so nice. He took his hand and shook it and said, "Oh, we've known Beverly for several years. She's a fine young lady," He went on and on. He really liked me, and he wished us well.

Lawrence, on the other hand, stood back and glared. He looked at this man with total contempt. I was completely astonished at his behavior, because he always was a gentleman. Never, never did I ever see Mr. Detroy behave as anything but a gentleman.

But when I introduced him to Lawrence, and my friend stuck out his hand to shake his hand, Lawrence turned on his heels and said, "Hnh!" and walked out the door!

Well, Frank was appalled. I was totally embarrassed. My friend was furious. I thought, "I don't understand what the problem is."

So after Frank made some excuse for Lawrence, he took off. My friend looked at me and asked, "Who is this Mr. Detroy?"

I said, "He's just a gentleman that I know here in the restaurant."

"Well, he really likes you, and I don't like him."

I chalked it up as an odd behavior on Lawrence's part and kind of tucked it away.

The next month or so, in dating this man, I began to see things that I didn't like. His behaviors and his true attitudes began to appear, and it became apparent to me that my mother saw more in this guy than I did, and that I would make a horrible mistake if I were to marry him. The clencher came when — well, never mind; I'm not going to talk about that.

We broke up.

I quit Murray State University after several years. I wasn't really interested in college, and I wasn't really pursuing it like I should. Plus, it was costing my family a lot of money. I decided I would go to work for Stouffer's full time where they offered me opportunities to develop skills and take different management courses and training courses that I really enjoyed. So I began to work at Stouffer's full time.

I watched a lot of women vie for Lawrence's attention. I got a kick out of it. I'd watch all the different lady friends he had. He was a bail-bondsman, and he had a bonding office with a secretary who was just beautiful. Her name was Kathy. I remember one time, Kathy had her aunt from Chicago come to Louisville with the thought in mind that she would fix this aunt up with Lawrence. She came to the dining room early one day and asked if I would make sure that, when their party was seated, I would seat Lawrence next to her aunt. When I replied, "Sure, no problem," she confessed her goal was to try to fix these two people up.

Well, when they arrived that day for lunch, Kathy's aunt was as pretty as she was, just a beautiful woman. She had jewelry and would be what you would classify as an elegant lady. God, she was gorgeous. I seated them all, and there must have been eight or nine people. I seated them all, but Lawrence refused to be seated. I left the chair empty for him to sit next to this lady. But all through the lunch, Lawrence would not sit down at the table.

He visited at this table, and he visited at that table. He talked to so-and-so, and somebody asked him something. He was all over the dining room. He was on the telephone making calls. He got calls. But he would not sit down at this table. The secretary became very agitated, and this stunning woman was embarrassed and fidgety.

I thought, "What is wrong with this man?"

So finally he got off the telephone, talking to somebody, and he came past me. I'm in the doorway of the dining room. I said, "Mr. Detroy, will you please sit down at the table?"

He said, "Why?"

"Well, your secretary's trying to fix you up with her aunt. You have to sit down next to her and try to carry on some kind of conversation."

He said, "I don't need to be fixed up. That's not who I like. And I am not going to sit down at that table." And he did not. So I thought, "Well, that's weird." She's beautiful — I mean stunning.

He never did sit at the table. He went over and passed a few words with everyone and laughed, but he never sat down. He made it apparent he was not a man to be fixed up with anybody.

It was aggravating to his secretary and funny to me, to watch him ignore what obviously everyone was trying to do. Kathy blamed me for it. I said, "I had nothing to do with it." I couldn't make the man sit. Later on I found out that at that time he liked me. His heart was for me. And I didn't know anything about it. I was trying to fix him up, or help fix him up, and I didn't know that.

A lot of women were interested in him. But I wasn't one of them. I lived at home with my parents and I did not drive a car. My father or my brothers would pick me up at work in the evening, and I would be driven to work by one of them. On a rare occasion I would take the bus. Usually I had a ride.

That afternoon, Lawrence was in the foyer making a phone call and he saw me getting ready to leave for the evening, and he wondered how I got back and forth to work. And he watched me as a car drove up out front. It was a station wagon. I opened the door to the vehicle, jumped in, hugged the man who was driving the vehicle, kissed him, and off we went.

Lawrence told me later that he thought, "I cannot believe that — she is dating an older man." He was shocked.

The next night, the same thing happens again. But Lawrence is waiting. He observes the same situation. I jumped in the station wagon, hugged this man, and off we went.

The third night, he decides he's going to follow us. He's in a vehicle, waiting for this station wagon to come up. And sure enough, the same thing happens again. Off we go. Lawrence follows us, all the way down Broadway, down Preston Street, to Standiford Lane, all the way down. He said, "I'll never forget, I'm thinking, 'What road is this?'" And the road went all the way to very end, pitch black. There was a park at the foot of the road, and we turned into this big, two-story house, and I leap out of the car and go running in. There are lights on all over the house, and there's people coming and going, and all kinds of racket. Lawrence writes down the license plate of the car. Since he was a bondsman and he was around court and was continually having to search down people, it was a simple matter for him to find out who this person was.

The following day he discovered that this man that I jumped in the car and hugged and kissed was my father.

I was totally unaware of any of this behavior. Or that I was even followed. In today's market, they'd call that "stalking." But I never considered Lawrence to be a stalker as such. During this period of my life, I wanted to get an apartment and be more independent, but the money that I was making at Stouffer's was not quite enough to support an apartment and sustain myself. So I decided I needed a part-time job, another job, a part-time job that would be just about enough to help me get over the hump to be able to live independently.

I checked around, but it was difficult to find something because the job I had was pretty time-consuming. I worked five days a week, and I worked fairly long hours there, so about the only thing that I could do would be something in the evening. Plus, I had to be careful of the kind of job I got because it had to suit my parents. They were both very strict.

I remember discussing with different people and letting them know I was looking for something. Then one day Lawrence stopped me and said he had a position for me, if I'd be interested. At Stouffer's I had been trained to do a wide variety of things, like cashiering and bookkeeping, and service classes, so I had the capability to do different things. Mr. Detroy said he needed a bookkeeper at night. I thought, "Oh! I could probably do that."

"Where is this? Where do you need me to be a bookkeeper?"

He had the bonding business. But he also had some nightclubs and a variety of places, so I honestly did not know what he was looking for. So he said he had a club and that it would be helpful if I could get there, say, at seven or eight o'clock at night, and straighten out the day's receipts. He bought a lot of liquor and beer and other items, and I could record all the invoices in the books and file them, and make the bank deposits.

I thought, "Well, I can handle that. I know how to do that, if he just shows me what he wants."

But I knew my parents would not approve of me working in a club. So I lied to them. I told them I had an extra little job that I'd be doing at Stouffer's.

The place where Lawrence wanted me to work was the Rooster Tail, which was a go-go club. Now, I did not drink and I had never been in any kind of club, much less a go-go club, so I was hesitant at first to do this. But he assured me that the time that I would be there would be before the club really opened, and that I would, after a couple of hours, be in a separate part of the building. I'd be able to leave quietly. I would not be subjected to the goings-on in the club, per se. That satisfied me. Plus, it was exciting.

I remember the first time I walked in that place. It was before it really opened. It was a nice little club, with bars and mirrors, and bar stools and cocktail tables. There was a stage, and there was an area where a band played.

On the wall, as you entered into the foyer of the Rooster Tail, were photographs of dancers. And in those days, go-go girls wore what would be the equivalent of a two-piece outfit. They were beautiful women. Most of them. There were some ugly ones too. But essentially most of them were very pretty.

Mr. Detroy takes me upstairs to an office and explains everything to me. He gives me the books, and I'm able to accomplish what it was he wanted. So I'm working at this place at night after I leave Stouffer's. I take a cab, leave Stouffer's, and go to the Rooster Tail. I do my work and slip out of the Rooster Tail before everything starts hopping.

Now this club was a popular meeting-place. Go-go clubs in those days were not for men only. This was a club that couples would come to, and conventioneers loved to come to this place. Downtown Louisville was a booming town and had a lot of conventions. A lot of people walked the streets, including couples. People would want to go to different types of clubs and get the flavor of the town. So we had probably as many women and couples as customers, as we had men.

Lawrence knew how to operate this club. He had a doorman — or usually he had two doormen on the front door. He had at least four waitresses, maybe five. He had a lot of dancers. He had a band called Grady and the Cats. And you could not tell what song this band was playing, because all their songs sounded exactly alike. One played the saxophone. There was a drummer. There was an organ player. Grady and the Cats were something.

There were black lights in the club. When a girl got up to dance, the black lights came on. Their costumes were a variety of colors, beaded and sequined, and everyone looked good under the black light. They looked even better if you had a few drinks in you!

Lawrence did not like the loud noise of the club, and he was known to be mainly standing out on the street in front of the club every night. He would hold conferences out on the street. Different other club operators would come by and see him. And he had other clubs downtown, too. Policemen would drive up. Taxicab drivers would drive up. People would park their cars, and they'd all stand around as the activities were going on in the club, with music and dancing and drinks being served. Lawrence would be out on the street, talking, and controlling everything in the club from out there.

He never approached me or never showed any interest in me other than as an employee. At that time I wasn't interested in him, either. But I was fascinated by the way he operated. He was always a gentleman.

One night he had problems with a waitress coming in late, and he asked me if I would come downstairs and help set the club up. And I thought, "Well, I can do that. That's easy." So I came downstairs, and I helped put out ashtrays and matches and set the tables, because a big convention had come to town. The two of us managed to get the club ready. Finally, the waitress came in, and was in time for the opening of the club. Then the rest of the help arrived.

I had a cocktail tray in my hand that I had used to carry over the various and sundry supplies that you needed for cocktail tables. He took the cocktail tray from me, and he said, "I want to go eat dinner, and I'd like for you to go with me."

I said, "No, I don't think so. I don't think that's appropriate. I'm not going with you."

He took the tray and put it up on a shelf. He said, "No, I don't want to eat by myself."

I said, "But I don't want to go anywhere with you. I'm just an employee, and I don't want to go."

He said, "Bev, please don't make me eat dinner by myself." I remember us fighting back and forth, because Lawrence was never anything other than a gentleman, and he never ever approached me about going out or being a date or anything like that — never. I always felt secure that he was a gentleman. Now all of a sudden he was insisting that I go out to dinner with him.

I'm still very young. On that particular night I was wearing a brown and white culotte dress. I'll always remember this dress, which was typical of the college fare that kids wore. He grabbed my coat, a pale yellow trench coat which was fashionable for kids but not fashionable for adults, and he pulled on my arm. I relented and decided rather than to argue with this man, okay, I would go with him, not knowing where we were going.

So we get into his car, which was a fancy gold Cadillac. I was dying a thousand deaths. I thought, "What am I doing in this car with this man? I cannot believe I'm getting stuck going out with him." I couldn't believe he was forcing me to go out with him. I guess I should have really put my foot down and said no. But in a way I did want to go.

So he takes me to a club, the Embassy Supper Club on Shelbyville Road. We drive up to the driveway and there's valet parking. There are gentlemen valet parkers in their tuxedoes. The valets came and opened the door of the car in front of us. A woman wearing a fur coat and a beaded dress comes out, and her husband on the other side. They're both dressed beautifully. I'm sitting in the car with a brown and white culotte dress and a yellow trenchcoat, and I'm dying. I'm thinking I cannot believe that I'm being put in this position.

I said, "Mr. Detroy, please don't take me to this place."

He said, "Oh, no, this is a really nice place. I'm friends with the owner, and you'll enjoy it. It's really nice."

He didn't understand the embarrassment it was for me. I was just totally humiliated. The next thing I know, the valet is opening my door and he's trying to get me to get out of car. But I was putting up a beef. I told him, "No, I don't think so. I think I'll stay in the car." I said to Lawrence, "You go eat and I'll wait in the vehicle."

Lawrence has no idea what my problem is. He said, "Come on, let's go!" The valet's pulling on my arm, so I get out of the car.

We go inside, and the club is just beautiful, with red velvet and plush carpeting and crystal chandeliers and soft music and candlelight. Everybody is elegant. It is just beautiful. And I am standing there in a brown and white culotte dress with a yellow trenchcoat dying ten million deaths. I thought I would just absolutely crawl in a hole and die.

So the maître d' tries to take my coat, and I say, "No. I'm leaving my coat on." I decided which would be worse: wearing my coat, or letting anyone see this awful cotton dress I had on.

Lawrence is not understanding what my problem is. I am totally humiliated. I pleaded, "Please don't make me sit in this place with you. Please. Just take me home. Take me back to the club. I've got work to do. Please don't put me in this position."

He said, "Look. If you're so embarrassed, we'll go sit in the side, in the corner."

So we get a little table that's off to the side, that's kind of dark, and I could not sit down fast enough. I'm thinking, "Oh, please, just let me get through this. This is *miserable!*" I'd never been so humiliated.

The waiter comes up. It was Jacques, the French waiter. And, oh, he had a thick accent, and he was, "Mademoiselle this" and "Mademoiselle that," and really playing it up. Of course Lawrence was familiar with everybody. All the servers and everybody knew him. The owner of the club comes over to where we were sitting. As years went on, I realized that Lawrence and the owner, Sam Pedro, were very good friends. But at this time I didn't really know what the relationship was. Sam was a ladies' man and liked to flirt a lot.

He sees Mr. Detroy with a very much younger woman, so he thinks he can flirt with me. Meanwhile I'm sitting there, totally humiliated, not even thinking in any manner like these men are thinking. So Lawrence gets upset with Mr. Pedro and orders him to the wine room. I'm sitting at the table. Jacques the waiter is trying to make me relax, trying to serve me escargots. I thought, "No way am I going to eat any escargots." I never drank, either, but he wanted me to have a glass of wine. I didn't want that; I wanted out.

Well, I hear this big commotion in the wine room, which is maybe twenty feet away from where we're sitting, and Lawrence is screaming bloody murder at this man, the owner of the club. Then they come out, and the owner is embarrassed. He comes over and apologizes for being out of line, for being over-friendly.

I remember getting through this dinner. And as we're leaving the club, I couldn't get out of there quick enough. It was a beautiful dining room and the food was elegant, but I couldn't enjoy one ounce of it. I was so totally humiliated. I thought, "I'll never get in a vehicle with this man again and I'm never, never going to get put in this position again. Just get me back to the club, let me do my work, and I'm going home."

That was our first date. That was my first date with Lawrence Detroy. We went for quite a while after that without going out. I just would go to work for him, do my thing, and go home. Eventually we began to relax enough that I could trust him, and I made him understand why I was so uncomfortable that night when we went out, and he just hadn't thought about it. He hadn't understood the humiliation that it was for me. I began to realize that he had been ignorant of that and that he was not mean-spirited in his behavior. He honestly wanted my company.

True Commitment

As a nurse, I look around and I see many people and many different relationships. I have the privilege of taking care of a lot of people when they are in very bad shape. I watch the interactions of couples. I'm forever fascinated with how people meet and how they have been loyal to one another over the years. I think my favorite thing is to ask an elderly couple how long they've been married, and then how did they first meet, and get them to tell me about their relationship. And the thing that I notice with people who are truly in love with one another is a common thread. It's the great respect and understanding for one another that they have. And I feel fortunate that I've been able to have that type of a relationship with a man. Although our time was maybe short to some people and long to others, Lawrence and I were really very fortunate in that we were able to have a loving relationship and a very fulfilled relationship.

When we began dating, there was a bit of a controversy over our age difference. My parents were absolutely infuriated by it. A lot of people didn't quite understand because it was such a big age difference. But I never thought about it. It was not of any concern to me that he was "X" amount of years older than me. I think that my heart was pure in my love for Lawrence, and also his for me.

We had dated perhaps three years or so when Lawrence and Frank had a little meeting. Frank really liked me. He really liked me. I was somebody he admired. He was concerned about our relationship and what it would do to my life and that it would destroy me.

I remember he and Lawrence sat down and discussed it, and Frank loved Lawrence, and he knew that Lawrence never would want to hurt me. He felt it was imperative that Lawrence front the situation and really think carefully about what would happen to this young woman's life if he continued on at the rate we were going. Lawrence was a very good man, and he loved me so much he did not want to see my life destroyed.

I'll always remember a time he picked me up for dinner, and we went to the Embassy Supper Club. It was the first place we ever ate together. This time, we ordered dinner, and he proceeded to go into this long tangent about our age difference. First off, was I aware that there was a tremendous age difference? Of course, I was aware of that.

He went on and explained to me that I deserved the right to have children, that I deserved and should have the right to have a life with someone who would not be notorious or would not be an embarrassment. He felt that if we continued on as we were and got married, then he would destroy me. It would destroy any opportunity that I would ever have to live what he and Frank "decided" was a happy life.

I remember sitting there listening to Lawrence, and it was very painful for him to say these things to me. I listened to him tell me all the things he and Frank had discussed and how they'd wisely decided my life for me. These two men who were so very caring just made me livid. I stood up at the table. Jacques the waiter came running over. "Is there a problem?"

And Sammy Pedro came running over. "Is something wrong?" I didn't speak to either one of them. I just walked to the door. The maître d' was there, and I asked him to get my coat. Then Jacques came running up to me, and Pedro came running after me, and Lawrence came running after me.

"What is wrong? What's wrong?" I couldn't speak to any of them. Finally, I asked the maître d' to get me a cab, and I wouldn't speak to Lawrence. I wouldn't speak to any of them. I was so furious at all of them. I could have thrown them all in the river. I walked out.

I had no money with me. I told the cabdriver Mr. Pedro would pay for the cab, and off we went. I went home.

I refused phone calls and I refused to see Lawrence or speak to him for anywhere from three weeks to a month after that. I would not. He sent word, he wrote letters, he did everything. I would not respond. Finally, I got a phone call from Frank. He said, "What are you so mad about that you won't even speak to Lawrence, or even to me?"

I said, "I'm not mad at either of you men." I explained, "I understand what you said, and I understand what you've done. But right now I don't want to speak to either one of you."

So, after about a month, Lawrence got me to agree to meet him. So we met. We sat down, and he couldn't understand my behavior. I said, "Well, I'll put it to you this way. You took my heart and then you put it in your pocket, and then you thought, or you think, that you can give it back to me. It's not quite that easy. You don't take somebody's heart and then turn around and hand it back to them on a plate. It doesn't work that way. I understand our age difference. I understand that. I understand the fact that we would never have children. I accept that. I understand that you have a lot of things that you've done that some people may say were bad and some people may say were good. All of that I'm aware of."

But none of that meant anything to me. What meant something to me was my love and my commitment to him. Not to Frank, not to his businesses, not to his car, not to any of the other stuff, but to the man. I saw in Lawrence things that I believe few people, except perhaps Frank, and maybe Frank's wife, JoAnn, saw, and that was a man who did the best he could do. He struggled, he fought, he used his wits and survived for himself and for his family and for his friends. Yet always he kept his integrity and his loyalty intact.

I saw these things in this man. I also saw the flaws and accepted them. I hoped that he would also see in me my flaws and accept them, and I felt if he was so weak that he didn't have the guts enough to understand that, then I didn't want him. But he still couldn't give me my heart back. He had my heart and he couldn't do that, and I wasn't about to accept it.

He was so amazed that I reacted that way. I guess both he and Frank thought I'd tuck tail and run. But it just didn't work that way with me. I've never been that way. And I found I've never regretted my decision to stay with Lawrence. I'm glad he had guts enough to realize that and to accept that as my decision, and my decision solely. That I realized our limitations in our relationship and accepted it. It was what I wanted, too. Sometimes you give up something to get something. And what I gave up, if you call it even giving up anything, didn't weigh nearly as much as what I gained in this relationship, which was all.

BACKGROUND: IRISH AND LEBANESE

Even though Frank Haddad and Lawrence Detroy were different, they were also a lot alike. You had one man that was educated bookwise, and one that was not. Both of them, though, came from the same era and the same type of upbringing. Above all, they loved their families and they believed in loyalty.

Their friendship was based on that loyalty. The saying, "You hold the lantern, while I dig the grave," was true of their friendship. They never, never flinched in the line of fire. It didn't matter which one was in trouble, Lawrence or Frank, or had problems; they stood for one another. That was an unspoken bond between them. That's one of the things that fascinated people about their relationship. That's the thing that has helped JoAnn and I to understand how these two men really appreciated one another. The ironic thing is that they were nine years apart in age, to the day. Both were born on June 23rd. That always fascinated me.

Here were two men raised in the Haymarket, one Irish and one Lebanese. Lawrence came from a family with bootleggers and gamblers. His Uncle Jack was a very powerful man who operated during the Depression era twenty-some speakeasies. People respected him, and a lot of people hated him. A lot of people loved him. He kept food on a lot of tables. He had a saying when Lawrence was a little boy: "A hundred dollars and a hundred days." If you got caught making gin in a tub by the authorities, you had to pay one hundred dollars and stay one hundred days in jail. "One hundred dollars, and one hundred days."

That wasn't a bad price to pay if you were starving, especially if you knew during the time that you were in jail, Uncle Jack, Lawrence's uncle, would make sure your family never went without food, and they remained on the payroll. So the members of these families that made gin for Uncle Jack would take turns who would be the one to go to jail. It didn't bother them. People loved Lawrence's Uncle Jack.

I have a newspaper clipping of when Uncle Jack died. The newspaper said it was the largest funeral procession in years. It showed a horse and carriage. It showed that people just loved Uncle Jack. Uncle Jack also controlled the political arena. Uncle Jack and Lawrence's family were Irish and Catholic.

Then you had the Haddad family, which was Lebanese. Frank's grandfather was of equal power and standing to Uncle Jack. They were in the meat business and the produce business, and Frank's grandfather controlled the Lebanese community. Their stores faced each other across the street. Uncle Jack's bar was on one side of the street, and Frank's family lived on the other side. They lived above their stores.

Frank's grandfather would come down every day and set an orange crate in front of his building, and sit down on it. He wore a white, starched shirt and supervised everyone during the day. You know, he was the Patriarch of the Lebanese.

Uncle Jack was an equal power for the Irish. They would have a problem in the bar and they'd come tumbling out. Farmers and people came from all around to the Haymarket. It was the market hub of Louisville. There would be problems. Someone would drink too much. They'd get into a fight. They'd start arguing over a card game or craps. They'd come tumbling out into the street.

The Lebanese men on the other side would get upset, because there'd be this big fight in the middle of the street. Frank's grandfather would signal to them to mind their own business — *unless* the other side, which was Uncle Jack, signified to him that he needed help. Then he'd say, "Okay," and then they'd all go tumbling in and straighten out whatever the thing was. But usually Uncle Jack's people could take care of their problems, and *vice versa* if there would be problems on the other side of the street. Uncle Jack would not interfere with the Haddads, unless he was asked to.

So they established a great respect. Politically you had Republicans and Democrats, and you had political wards. If you controlled all of these people making gin in tubs in all of these communities that were being fed, and if the Haddad family fed a lot of people, too, then you had a lot of votes.

When it came to election time, they could select who they wanted to put in office. They handpicked them. But they understood each other. Lawrence was a Democrat and Frank was a Republican through the years, but many people never knew which was which. Maybe most people knew Frank was a Republican, but they never could figure out what party Lawrence was, because he would show up at Republican functions *and* Democratic functions.

II. FAMILY HISTORY

Uncle Jack O'Hearn
"He'll Never Bother Me Again."
Burned
Johnny Weber's Element of Surprise: He Kicks Like a Mule
"Are You a Prophet?"
The License

Uncle Jack O'Hearn

Lawrence's Uncle Jack was a very powerful man, and he operated over twenty speakeasies in Louisville during the Depression era. Lawrence adored him. His Uncle Jack was his mother's brother. Jack O'Hearn was this man's name. He was very close to Lawrence's mother, Maggie Lee. Jack O'Hearn had many people around the city of Louisville making gin in tubs for his speakeasies.

He was well-loved. Essentially because, during this era, there was no work for anybody, and in order to eat, you had to have a job, and since there were no jobs, making gin in the tub became a welcome occupation.

The law fixed a punishment for people caught making gin in a tub. The judge would give you a hundred days in jail and a fine of one hundred dollars. But the people who made the gin accepted this as part of their job. And if they were caught, then the deal was that Uncle Jack would support their family while they did time in jail. So the family never went without groceries or food the entire time they were in jail. Uncle Jack would have his men deliver food and money to these families, so none of his employees was left starving during the punishment. They accepted this willingly as part of their work for Uncle Jack.

During this era, Chicago was booming with its speakeasies. And the club operators in one town would hear about the successes of another town, and they would try to expand operations into the other community.

Powerful people from Chicago decided Louisville was a booming town, and they decided they wanted to take over Uncle Jack's speakeasies.

Lawrence was a little boy at this time, but he remembered very well the rumblings and the gossip and the conversations about people being sent to Louisville to take over Uncle Jack's clubs. He said that two men got on a train in Chicago and rode down to Louisville on the train. They were hit men. Their plan was to come to Louisville and assassinate Lawrence's uncle. Then their organization from Chicago would move in and take over the Louisville speakeasies.

The thing these men didn't understand was that Uncle Jack, who had people placed all over Louisville, who had so many people on his payroll, had friends everywhere. If you didn't work for Uncle Jack, you had a friend who worked for him or a family member who worked for him. He was a really well-liked man, and one of the people on the train was a conductor who liked Uncle Jack. He picked up on the gameplan of these two men.

When he got to the Louisville train station, the conductor contacted somebody who contacted Uncle Jack, to inform him that these two hit men had arrived in Louisville. Lawrence was with his uncle, and he was just a little boy, and he remembered men coming to Uncle Jack and telling him something. They were all excited, and he picked up a little bit of the conversation. Being a kid, he was able to maneuver in and out and around people, and people really didn't pay attention to him. He heard them saying something about someone trying to kill his uncle. His Uncle Jack was very calm, and he looked at him and said, "Now, Lawrence, you stay here. I'll be back in a few minutes." And he left.

After a couple of hours, Uncle Jack came back, and they went on doing what they had been doing. Lawrence would go with his Uncle Jack when he would make his stops, and collect money, and do all the different things that he did.

The next day, through the rumor mill, Lawrence heard that two men had been shipped back to Chicago in a pine box, and he knew that his Uncle Jack had killed these two hit men.

This result did not go over too well with the man who sent these hit men to Louisville. And so, several weeks later, the Chicago people sent two other men down to do the job. These men traveled to Louisville in a private vehicle. But Louisville, although a booming town, was essentially a small town. It was apparent when there was a stranger in town.

When these two men arrived, it was common knowledge that they were in town to assassinate Lawrence's uncle, and that the community was opposed to that. People were acutely aware of these strangers. And, some way or another, they became certain what these two men were up to. Then the community stopped the strangers from killing Lawrence's uncle. One man was killed, and the other was given the responsibility of taking the body back to Chicago. After that, there were no more attempts to take over the Louisville speakeasies. An agreement was reached that Louisville was off the map as far as this organization was concerned. It wasn't worth the trouble. It wasn't so lucrative that it would compensate for the trouble to keep trying to get this man.

When Lawrence's uncle did die, the newspapers said it was the longest funeral procession in Louisville to date at that time. This man was a strong man and well-loved, even though some people may have looked at him and thought he was a bad person.

But this was the man Lawrence looked up to and admired as a child. He got a lot of his wits and his ability to roll with the blows from observing his Uncle Jack.

Lawrence had three brothers. His oldest brother was named after Uncle Jack, Jack Gogan; his next brother was Tom Gogan, and then there was Jerry Gogan. When their father died, Lawrence's mother married Rudolph Detroy. Then Lawrence came along, and Ethel. There were two other sisters, too: Pat, and I forget the other one. She's still alive.

The four brothers were very loyal to one another, and Lawrence said you never did anything to one of them without harming all of them. During the era they were brought up in, they stuck together. Everybody knew that these brothers were loyal to one another and, although they may have bickered among themselves, they stood up for each other.

Tom was a terrible gambler, and they had a lot of problems with him. Jerry was extremely violent. He had the hottest temper. He married a woman named Bernice, who was Rufus Allen's sister, who later on married another really nice man. But Jerry was a very violent man, and they were forever having problems with him and his temper.

As brothers, they were all unique. Lawrence was the youngest of the four, yet he was more or less the leader as he grew up. He could figure out situations and come up with concepts and ideas on how to make a living. These men all had families, and they all wanted to make a living and survive. They bootlegged. They ran gambling casinos. They did a variety of things. They traveled across the country "crossroad hustling." But everything they did was for survival and to protect and provide for the family.

Lawrence's oldest brother, Jack, ran a club located directly across the street from the Haddad meatmarket. The Haddad family lived above the meatmarket.

When Lawrence was thirteen or fourteen, a lot younger than his brother Jack, he thought that his oldest brother had gone crazy. Everybody did. It was the dead of winter, and yet his brother made him take a squeegee and squeegee off the window of the bar while he stood in the window and he moved his hands about. Lawrence said, "I remember looking at my brother and thinking, 'Oh man, he's nuts! He's gone nuts. He's flipped out!'" Jack was strong-willed and had a lot of idiosyncrasies. He was an amateur photographer. He pretended to be a doctor. He read medical books. He always had a lot of odd ways about him.

But Jack had fallen in love with Frank Haddad's aunt, Frank's father's sister, and that was considered terrible because this was the Lebanese and the Irish. Jack's reputation as a bar owner and gambler and a racketeer didn't fit into what the Haddad family wanted for Nellie. But Nellie fell in love with Jack also. It was a great love story. Jack had taught her sign language, and because they were forbidden to see each other, she would sit in the window of her bedroom, and they would communicate back and forth through the night. Lawrence's job during the winter, when the windows would steam up, was to squeegee the steam off the window so that Jack could talk to Nellie. Later on this came out, but at the time, as a little boy, Lawrence thought, "My brother is nuts."

Eventually Nellie and Lawrence's oldest brother did get married. Although it wasn't accepted, and people were very upset in both the Irish *and* the Lebanese communities, they finally came to terms with the fact that these two people loved one another and had to be married. Jack was very dedicated to Nellie to the point that he was so protective and possessive of her through their entire marriage, that nobody was permitted to visit in their house. Even Lawrence seldom visited. "I would go there," he said, "but it was very rare." These two really, really loved each other. They had two children, Larry Gogan and Glen Gogan, and Larry recently passed away.

Lawrence remembered Frank Haddad when they were little. Lawrence was exactly nine years to the day older than Frank Haddad, and they were both born June the 23rd. Lawrence said he remembered Frank as a young man, and Frank was a wrestler, and he could fight. He was a wrestler or a boxer. But even though Frank was little, he could defend himself pretty well. He worked hard for his dad in the meat store.

Frank's father was so strong and so big. And Frank's mom, Clara, was an Italian lady and just the sweetest-natured woman. Big Frank was very powerful and had a booming voice. A lot of people were afraid of him. But Lawrence always said his bark was a lot worse than his bite. Big Frank's heart was big. He was a compassionate man, but he didn't want people to know it. He would get very upset if a meat preparer would try to cheat him with the weights of the meat, or in some other way.

Frank's wife, JoAnn, told me about her first visit to the Haddad house above the meatmarket. Frank's father was there. And somebody had apparently tried to cheat Big Frank on the delivery of some meat. There was a fan in the living room, and he was furious. He was screaming and yelling about the person that tried to cheat him, and he picked up the fan and flung it. JoAnn was just walking past the window, and the fan went out the window, right past JoAnn's head. This was her first impression of Big Frank! She had a lot of respect for this guy. She found out later he was really a good person.

Frank's mother was much more gentle and soft. Lawrence said when he would take his sons to the Haddad meatmarket, the kids, their children, would always want to go, because when they got there, Clara Haddad would slip them a little hot dog or a piece of bologna. She would always give them something. Usually, it was a hot dog. It was a kind thing to do. I've heard the same story repeatedly from many, many different people. She didn't do it for fanfare. The children loved this sweet woman who loved children.

Big Frank would be weighing the meat and giving customers advice about how to prepare the food and meat, but all the children adored Frank Haddad's mother. Frank's mom and dad ran the meat store because they liked people. They liked to see people as families, and with their children.

"He'll Never Bother Me Again."

Lawrence told me a few stories about himself as a little boy. The thing that always amazed me about Lawrence was his continual ability to not give up and to fight. This was something as a child he was taught by his parents. He had the natural ability to be a scrapper, and that sustained him throughout his life.

When he was a little boy around Louisville, there was a policeman who was a beat officer. I can't remember the man's name. I know Lawrence used to say "Officer So-and-So," but I cannot remember what his name was. This policeman was very mean and cruel to people. A policeman could be like that in those days. Citizens were at the mercy of bad policemen. Now our rights are more explicit. He would take his billy club and hit you if you were somebody he didn't like. A group of kids could be standing together and he'd be walking by with his club, and he would hit one of the kids.

Lawrence had a newspaper stand. He would stand on the corner and sell newspapers. This policeman would sometimes knock his stand over or chase him from the corner. He was a mean fellow. He was mean to a lot of people, not just the kids. If he ever got the chance to bully anybody, he would. Even as a little boy, Lawrence despised this man. Almost everybody he knew despised this man. They'd see him coming, and usually they would scatter or run, because they knew that he would, one way or another, hurt them.

Lawrence was little, maybe eleven or twelve. And for years this man had made vicious comments and cracks to Lawrence and his brothers, and to his friends, about them being "ragpickers" and so on, because they were poor. Lawrence had such contempt for this man, and he thought to himself, "Someday I'll get even with this fellow."

One day, a tremendous storm rained down on Louisville. The day before, this officer had done something to his newspaper stand that had cost him. Lawrence lost all of the stand. This policeman's act really devastated Lawrence, a little boy, and cost him the money he made selling newspapers that helped feed the family. Lawrence was always proud to take money to his mother so they could buy things. It was hard to find work, and anytime you could contribute to the family, it really was a wonderful thing. But this officer interrupted that and had interfered with Lawrence and his ability to help his family.

On this particular day, it was raining sheets. And this officer had a car. Most of the time he'd park the car and walk the beat. But this day he was in the car, and Lawrence was on a bike. He rode up beside this man in the car. It was pouring down rain, and Lawrence jeered him. And the officer was furious at him. Lawrence hollered at him, said some things to him, and then he took off on his bike.

The officer in his vehicle proceeded to follow Lawrence on his bike. Lawrence was skinny and wimpy, but he was fast. He pedaled as fast as he could, and the guy's car followed him. Lawrence knew where he was going. He rode on deliberately. He swerved in and out of streets and up alleys and down alleys, and the policeman kept right with him. Every opportunity he could get away with it, he'd stop and jeer this man. Finally the boy came to a hill that was in the Highlands.

The street on this hill in the Highlands dips down very straight. It's a cobblestone street. It's still cobblestone, or it was until a few years ago. The street is very, very severe and dips straight down, through the whole block.

Lawrence got to this particular part of the Highlands and he jeered the officer, and he turned onto this street. By that time, the officer had accelerated to keep up with Lawrence and was adamant to catch him. He was going to catch this little boy and probably beat him, if he could get hold of him. Lawrence made a turn on this street to the left and then suddenly swerved toward the first yard on the left, and went up the driveway to the back of the house.

The car turned to the left also, but the only thing was, he couldn't stop, and he went skidding down the hill. The hill dropped straight down and was cobblestone, and the policeman lost control of his vehicle. At the foot of the hill, the rain had caused flooding, and this officer's vehicle went straight down into a watery culvert. That was the end of that officer.

Lawrence said, "I remember as a little boy coming out of the driveway on my bike and looking down and seeing that car headfirst in this culvert of water, river of water, and thinking, 'He'll never bother me again.'"

I know that sounds cruel, but what this man did to the people in this community was more cruel. That was an example of how Lawrence had to and did survive. He knew this man was vicious enough to chase him. He knew he was vicious enough to try to catch him and hurt him. He also knew the man was stupid and would follow him. He said, "I've never regretted that that man died that way."

BURNED

Prohibition existed during the year that Lawrence was born, which was 1919, until it officially ended in 1933. So throughout his youth prohibition and its opposing forces dominated activity in this country. By the time Lawrence was ten years old, the nation was beset by a post-war fear of communism and radicals. Dictatorships were springing up all over the world and in Europe. This country had a sense of fear. One little rumor could spread like wildfire and grow bigger and bigger with every telling of the story.

The women, including Lawrence's mother and the mothers of the neighborhood, would frequently gather together and sit on their front stoops and talk about what was happening in the community. The children would run and play and get in trouble.

Lawrence was always in trouble as a child. And he had no fear. He was the youngest of the brothers, but he was always the leader in deciding things to do. When somebody would ask him to do something, even something considered dangerous, he was the first to volunteer.

One day when he was about ten years old, right after church, a group of boys talked him into an extremely dangerous act. Lawrence had on his new pair of knickers and Sunday clothes. He had two sets of clothes, everyday clothes and his Sunday clothes. The families were very poor, and the people treasured their Sunday clothes. They would take them off after church like prized possessions.

This day, instead of going home after church, Lawrence met with a group of these boys, who were mostly older. They lifted up a manhole cover, and they dangled Lawrence by his ankles and lowered him into the sewer. They had a carbide canister, an explosive device. It was Lawrence's job to take the lid off this canister.

Lowered into the sewer, he took the lid off the canister. Instantly, the gas of the sewer and this carbide exploded. It's a miracle the blast didn't kill Lawrence and the kid holding him. But it blew the manhole cover down the block, and it cracked the street for the full block. All of the kids flew. They scattered. The two boys at the manhole, Lawrence and the older boy, took off. Their clothes were burned to smithereens. Lawrence's clothes were all totally black, and burned, and in shreds. Here he is, this little boy, who knows he's going to get in trouble when his mother sees his clothes.

He sneaked home, went in the back door, and took off his burned and shredded clothes. He took a bath, washed himself, rolled up his clothes in butcher paper, and hid them up in the attic. Then, for the following three Sundays, instead of going to church with his mother and the family, he woke up early in the morning and went to the earliest Mass offered at that time. Then he would come home and tell his mother, "I've already been to church. I went to Mass." His mother always checked with the priest, and sure enough, they acknowledged Lawrence did what he said. Lawrence's mother, Maggie Lee, was a smart lady, and she knew something wasn't quite right for this little boy to get up so early to go to Mass. Prior to this, she'd had to drag him out of bed to go to Mass with her.

When the street blew up, the community was sure it was an attack from a foreign country and sabotage, and that somebody was trying to take over this country. The rumors ran rampant that amongst the people there was an enemy. And the story kept getting bigger and bigger and bigger. As a little boy, Lawrence would go by the different stoops, and he'd hear the women and the men, and they'd all be talking about that bombing and so on. This mischievous act by two boys turned into an act of sabotage. The kids didn't know what to do; they were scared to death. The story kept getting bigger and bigger and bigger, because fear was running rampant in this country. The juicy story just got juicier and juicier.

Finally, after several weeks, Lawrence's suspicious mother said, "Lawrence, I want to see your Sunday clothes." She figured he'd done something to his Sunday clothes. Lawrence hem-hawed around. But she insisted, "Get me the Sunday clothes now!" So Lawrence went and got the clothes rolled up in butcher paper and brought it down and handed it to his mother.

His mother laid this rolled-up sack of butcher paper on the kitchen table. She unrolled it on the table. In the middle of the sack, she found the knickers and the little suit and shoes that were just torn to shreds. They were burned. And she instantly knew the culprit who had blown up the sewer a couple of blocks away. She quietly rolled up the clothes in the sack and disposed of it, and she told Lawrence to keep his mouth shut. She never mentioned it to him again. Of course, the rumors still continued to spread about the sabotage bombing and more to come, but she never admitted her ten-year-old little boy had exploded the sewer. She feared what would happen to them, because this was really considered an act of sabotage.

During the early 1900s, mothers had a difficult time correcting their children. Lawrence in particular was an adventurous little boy who got into lots of trouble, and his mother forever tried to figure out a way to control his behavior. One technique that was commonly used by mothers in those days was to put a dress on her son if she wanted to keep the child in the yard. It was thought the embarrassment of him wearing a dress would prevent him from leaving the yard, and that he would stay and behave himself in his yard or his house or wherever he was confined.

This tactic worked with Maggie Lee's other boys. She was able to control their behavior. They learned that if they didn't behave, they would suffer this humiliation, so they would mind a lot. But Lawrence was different. When she put a dress on him, he blatantly walked out in the middle of the street. The first kid to say something would be popped in the nose, and that would be the end of it.

A friend who grew up with him, said, "I can remember, Lawrence would get out in the middle of the street and play kickball and play as hard as anybody else, and Lord help any of us if we commented about the dress, because he would bop us in the head!"

Johnny Weber's Element of Surprise: He Kicks Like a Mule

Johnny Weber was famous around the Haymarket during the early days when Lawrence was a little boy. He was ten or fifteen years older than Lawrence, and he was friends with Lawrence's older brothers. He took a liking to the Fox, and decided to be his mentor. He was very protective of Lawrence.

Weber was a little man in stature, but he was known for his ability to fight. He worked around the produce market. He owned fruit stands and delivery trucks. But his true living came from being a bookmaker and a gambler. Mainly a bookmaker. He had clubs. He was a likable little guy. He was funny. And the fact that he was so little sometimes made bullies want to pick on him.

The first time Lawrence was in Weber's company was in a bar. They were getting ready to "shoot craps." They were going to shoot craps, and some enormous man, twice Weber's size, decided he wanted to pick a fight. And of course he picked the littlest guy in the bar. He knows he can win a fight with him. The big guy starts mouthing off and bragging how he's going to hurt this little guy and so on. Lawrence was really worried. Weber just sat there, ignoring the guy. He just sat there, and he had a drink in his hand. He'd take a sip and just stare straight ahead and not say a thing or do anything. Lawrence finally said, "Weber, you know, that man over there is talking about hitting you."

And Weber said, "Yeah, I know. I heard him." The other guy went on, and he was mouthing off. He made fun of Weber's size, and he walked up closer to Johnny. It was so fast. Johnny spun around in the chair and hauled off and hit him so hard in the jaw that he knocked the guy out cold. Then he turned back around in his chair and continued to drink his drink.

Lawrence said, "Johnny, I can't believe you did that!"

And Weber said, "The element of surprise. It will help you in most battles."

As the years went on, as Lawrence was in different situations, he saw Weber do this repeatedly. He was known for this. Johnny had long arms, and he had a powerful punch. He would wait like he did with this big fellow until a guy thought he had total advantage of Johnny because he didn't even acknowledge he was there, and then he would hit them when they'd least expect it, the instant before they'd get an opportunity to hurt him. Lawrence saw very few times where Weber lost a battle in all the years he was around him, unless there were multiple people picking on him. And then, others had to jump in to help Johnny. But in most cases, Weber could take care of himself.

Johnny Weber's hit was like the kick of a mule. People agreed, "He kicks like a mule." He would take his whole body and put it into a punch, swing his arm back and his entire body would follow his fist as he went forward and hit people. Weber's hit was like a mule kicking you.

"Are You a Prophet?"

When Lawrence was a teenager, he came down with a disease that was common in that era — tuberculosis. Tuberculosis was a killer. There was no true cure for TB, with the exception of rest and doing pneumothoraxis, where they collapsed your lungs and allowed the lesions on your lungs to heal, and trying to diet. You had to go on total bed rest, breathe fresh air, and deflate your lungs enough to permit the lesions to heal and to stop hemorrhaging.

Lawrence was a teenager, and he had the dreaded disease. It was so common, people were dropping like flies. Most people who got tuberculosis didn't make it. Most died. Lawrence was about sixteen years old, and his mother was very concerned about him.

His poor health was apparent. He lost weight and was having night sweats. He was suffering a tremendous amount. He really, really struggled with TB. His mother was terribly concerned, especially because Lawrence was bucking the system and didn't want to comply with the medical advice for treatment. Treatment for TB was severe, requiring total bed rest and fresh air. But he didn't go home at night. He hung out around the Haymarket and refused to follow the doctors' orders that his mother wanted him to do.

His good friend was Johnny Weber, who had a produce stand. Johnny Weber saw this young kid, whose nickname was "Slim" because he was so skinny, who had no stamina, who was weak, and who would start coughing until he hemorrhaged and coughed up blood. That was a very severe sign he was in terrible shape. Weber tried to encourage him to eat. He got him to drink wine, hoping to build up his strength. Lawrence would drink a glass of red wine at every meal. Probably that was one of the things that sustained him, because that encouraged him to eat. This was homemade wine, and it helped him.

One morning early, Lawrence had been out. He didn't go home. Weber found him in a pile somewhere along the Haymarket, where he had just collapsed. He was lying in a pool of blood and they couldn't get him awake. He was pretty lethargic. They rushed him to the hospital. He was just a teenager, maybe sixteen or seventeen years old, and they felt like he was dying. So they sent him immediately to Waverly Hills, which was the major hospital that took care of these patients at this time. If you drive out on Dixie Highway sometime, you can look up in the hills and see it. It's an enormous, humongous stone building.

They take him to Waverly Hills, and they put him in the hospital. They determined he was in stage terminal, and there was nothing more that could be done for him.

Lawrence said, "I opened my eyes. I could hear this crying sound." It was his mother, standing over the bed, and there was a priest standing over him. They were doing the last rites. All the family — the mother, Maggie Lee, in particular — was crying and wailing about the loss of her son.

Lawrence was very weak, but he was able to speak. He asked her what she was crying about, and she said, "Well, the doctor told me you probably won't make it through the night." Then she just started sobbing, like a mother would, with a broken heart at the thought of losing her son.

Lawrence lay in that bed and looked at all these people around him and thought, "Now this is ridiculous." He said, "You all, help me get up." He was so weak, he could barely walk.

They all pleaded, "No, no, no, Lawrence, you can't get up! You've got to lie in the bed! You can't get up!"

He said, "Help me get up!"

So they got him to stand up, and he put a robe on, and he said, "Where is the doctor's office?" They told him. Waverly Hills is an enormous place, and it has long corridors, like close to half a mile long. The doctor's office was at the end of the corridor down another hallway, about halfway. It was a substantial distance for somebody as weak and ailing as Lawrence was. But he said, "I'm going to go see him." The nurses were fighting him. Everybody there was trying to discourage him, but Lawrence was stubborn and demanding. He said, "I'm going!" So they let him go.

"I thought I'd *never* get to that doctor's office," he said. "I'd take a few steps, and I'd have to take a breath. I'd take a few more steps, and I'd take a breath. And then I'd start coughing. I'd cough and, I'll always remember, I had a little emesis basin with me, and I'd spit up blood. I had Kleenexes. I'd wipe my mouth, and then I'd take some more steps. It probably took me twenty or thirty minutes to get to that doctor's office." He said, "Nurses were stopping me; they were saying, 'You've gotta get in bed! You're not allowed to do this!'"

And the way they operated this hospital, the people had to follow orders. But he wasn't going to listen any of them. He was adamantly stubborn, and he gets all the way to the doctor's office. The nurse is already ahead of him, saying that this patient is boycotting and he's refusing to comply, and so on. Everybody's upset with Lawrence. He collapses in the doctor's arms. The doctor takes him in the office and sits him in the chair. And he asks, "What in the hell do you think you're doing, young man?"

And Lawrence said, "I want to ask you a question, doctor."

"What?"

"Are you God?"

And the doctor answered, "Well, of course I'm not God!"

"Well, are you a prophet?"

"Well, of course I'm not a prophet! I'm a doctor!"

"Then I want you to go down that hallway and tell that woman who's standing over my bed crying, thinking I'm not going to make it through the night, that you don't know *when* I'm going to die! You or nobody knows, only God does." And he said, "You tell her that! I don't want her standing over me, crying like that." He said, "I happen to have a lot more fight in me than you even know."

He had to have fight to get to the doctor's office. The doctor could see this. They ended up getting a wheelchair and taking him back to his bed. The doctor spoke to the mother and confirmed what Lawrence wanted him to do. He admitted he didn't know when Lawrence would die. He said, quite frankly, somebody who had that much gumption and that much fight probably wouldn't die.

As time went on, Lawrence survived the tuberculosis. He and this doctor became dear friends. And whenever they would see each other, the doctor would say, "No, I am not a prophet!"

The doctor died before Lawrence did, as a matter of fact. That's an example of the fighter Lawrence was, all of his life. Whenever people would say something like, "Well, this is it. It's over. The party's over. You've lost the battle," that's when Lawrence would get the roughest and the toughest. That's when he would fight the hardest.

THE LICENSE

Lawrence was a bondsman. As a bondsman he ran through a large variety of people. There was a little guy who would come into the bonding office who had a lot of children. He had five or six kids. The guy worked around for other people. He did electrical work, a little plumbing work, and just anything that needed to be done. He was an assistant who would help other people, builders and contractors, to make a living for his family.

One day this man came into Lawrence's bonding office. He was a real sweet man. He said, "Mr. Detroy, I need your help."

Lawrence said, "Well, sure. What do you need?" He knew he was a good fellow. He'd had a few little problems. Lawrence got him out on drunk driving. But we all have problems, so you just have to deal with it.

The guy said, "I want to get my license to be an electrician."

And Lawrence said, "No problem."

Big Frank Haddad was Building Inspector, and he was the one who issued licenses to plumbers and electricians. This was a political position that Frank's father had. His office administered the test. The office was naturally downtown.

Lawrence and Big Frank liked one another. Lawrence really liked Big Frank Haddad. They had great respect for each other.

Lawrence said, "No problem," he said, "I'll take you to Mr. Haddad's office, and you can go ahead and get the electrician test. No problem," he reassured him. "I'll introduce you to the man."

The little guy said, "Well, yeah, there is a problem."

"What's that?"

"I can't read."

"You *what*?"

"I can't read."

"Well, how in the hell are you going to take the test?" asked Lawrence.

"I know everything. If you ask me the questions, I can give you the answers."

Lawrence knew Big Frank would not like this, but he liked this guy. He was trying so hard. He wanted to provide for his family. This was a way to do that. If he could get a license, he could have his own business. He could be independent. He could provide for his family. Big Frank was known for his hot temper, and so was Lawrence. But they had great respect for each other, so he took the man over to Haddad's office.

Lawrence went right in the office. He had the man wait out in the waiting room. Lawrence went back and told Big Frank his problem. He said, "I have a guy that wants to try and get an electrician license."

Big Frank said, "Well, no problem, Fox, bring him in!"

Lawrence said, "Well, yeah, there's a little problem."

"What's that?"

"The guy can't read or write."

Well, Big Frank blew up. He was very gruff, very rude. "Goddammit, Lawrence! What the hell do you mean bringing a man to me who can't read or write? How the hell am I going to give him the test?"

"Hold it, hold it, hold it... wait," said Lawrence. "Now, listen to me. He knows this stuff. Just is it a law that you have to handwrite the answers?"

Big Frank sat there and said, "Well, I don't think so."

"Well, *ask* him the questions out loud! And *see* if he knows them!" So Big Frank relented and agreed. It wasn't against the law.

So they bring the guy in, and Lawrence leaves and goes and sits out in the waiting room, and Frank proceeds to give this man the electrician's test orally. The man knew everything. The guy spouted out the answers perfectly. He passed. He got his license. Big Frank gave him a license, and the guy was so grateful. "Thank you, thank you, *thank you*, Mr. Haddad.

Thank you, thank you, Mr. Detroy. Oh, I really appreciate it." He was just totally grateful. It meant everything to this man.

Big Frank said to the guy, "I want to tell you. Don't *ever* put me in this position again. If I see you again, I want you to know how to read. I want you to learn to read."

The new electrician took off. For several years, Lawrence would see the fellow and wave at him, and he'd wave back. Lawrence would ask him how he was doing, and he'd say, "I'm doing great," and "Everything's fine." He would always say, "I appreciate everything. Thank you. I appreciate what you did for me."

Several years later, this fellow showed up in Lawrence's office again. Lawrence thought the guy had the same look on his face as he did that day when he wanted Lawrence to help him get the license. Lawrence looked up and wondered, "Oh Christ, what's wrong now?"

Big Frank was still Building Inspector, and still in charge of all the tests. So this fellow said, "Mr. Detroy, I need your help again."

Lawrence said, "What?"

"Uh, Mr. Detroy? I've gotta make a trip to go see Mr. Haddad."

He said, "I want to take the plumber's test." He said, "If I could do the plumbing, get a license for plumbing, in addition to electrician, then I'd *really* have a nice business."

Lawrence said, "Oh, my God! I can't believe you're putting me in this position. Please don't make me go over there and see Big Frank! I did it once. I went through the fire for you."

The guy said, "I'm telling you, I want you to walk me over to the office and take me in there. I need you to go with me."

Lawrence relented, "I'll do it. But I don't know how Frank's going to react. I want to tell you, he'll probably blow up. He'll kill us both!"

The man pleaded, "I insist. I want you to go with me to get my plumber's license. This is important."

The man was adamant. The guy was gentle-natured. For him to be that determined, Lawrence admired that. He took the fellow over to Frank's office.

They go in. Big Frank sees this man, and he blows sky-high. "What do you want? What are you doing? What's wrong now?"

"Well, I want to take the plumber's license."

Big Frank exploded. "Now look! I helped you once. I helped you get the electrician's license." He spread his big hands on his desk. "Granted, you knew everything. But I bent the rules a little bit!" And he carried on and screamed.

Lawrence said, "I'm going. But Frank, the guy's a family man! He's got these kids." But Big Frank kept exploding.

Finally the little electrician said, "Would you two please be quiet for a minute? I have something I want to say."

So they both shut up.

"What?"

"This time I want to take the test in writing, because in the few years that I've been away from you all, I've learned how to read and write."

The man took the test, and he passed.

That was an example of how people helped each other. They bent the rules for this little guy, so he took the first test and passed. He was smart. The man took what they did for him and bettered himself.

Here was a little guy who could not get a break. But because two people took the time to help him, he took the incentive to learn to read and write. That may not sound like much. But that was the true essence of Big Frank Haddad and Lawrence Detroy and Little Frank Haddad — all of them. They loved to help people, to help them help themselves. They never turned their backs.

III. GANG

Seeing Good Beneath the Surface
The Greenville Trial
Senator Cook Waits
Friends
Sebastiani Winery
San Francisco Trolley Ride
Chinatown Fight
Piña Colada
The Glass of Wine

SEEING GOOD BENEATH THE SURFACE

People who traveled with Frank knew how he was. Frank and Lawrence both loved people. They loved a challenge. They loved an underdog.

If somebody said, "This person can't be helped," those two guys would get in after them. It was just their way. They both had "wards of the state" as people who were alcoholics or had mental problems or whatever were called. But they were always loyal to them.

A poem was read at Lawrence's funeral that had been written by Jimmy Wilson.

Jimmy was a lowly alcoholic people would step over, shove to the side. He was a mental case who absolutely loved Lawrence. Lawrence was kinder to him than his own father. And to think that poetry would come from this little person seems impossible. But Lawrence and Frank could see that. They could see it in people where others couldn't. They weren't impressed by people with power or money. They weren't impressed by anything except genuine sincerity and loyalty.

The Greenville Trial

When Frank took the murder case down in Greenville, his father, Big Frank, was very upset. It meant Frank had to go out in the state to a town that was known to be the Ku Klux Klan center, literally, in Kentucky.

Big Frank knew, and was acutely aware, that it was dangerous for Frank to go down to this town to represent this client. The situation was particularly terrible because the two most prominent citizens of the community, a dry county, had been murdered — the bootleggers.

Greenville has always been a Southern town where the Civil War has continued on. And the accused murderers were two black men, accompanied by a woman who was from the North. A white woman.

She was white *and* she had a child, and she left the child in New Jersey, where her parents were. They were fairly wealthy and very devastated over this girl's behavior.

The girl somehow picked up with the two men. And together, they traveled through the South. They learned about these bootleggers, and they went up to the bootleggers' place at the top of a hill to this big house. The girl sat in the automobile, while the two black men went up to the bootleggers under the pretense of buying liquor. They shot the bootleggers with a shotgun and killed them both. It wasn't long before they were apprehended.

The family contacted Frank to represent their daughter. A black attorney named Aubrey Williams had the unfortunate responsibility of representing the two black men. Aubrey laughed because he said he knew he was in trouble. All three defendants were tried at the same time. On the first day of trial, they had two tables joined for the defense. The table was for Frank, this girl, Aubrey Williams, and the two men. Frank walked into the courtroom and he said, "Fox, let's move these tables apart." And they separated the tables.

Aubrey said he knew he was in trouble because he had hoped to ride on the coattails of Frank Haddad. But it was clear right away that Frank was there to represent *his* client. *His* client would not look good sitting at the table with the two black men in this community that despised blacks with whites to start with. Not to mention people from the North. One was as bad as the other, in a place like Greenville.

There was so much publicity, and so much hatred, about this particular case in the community. On the first day of trial, they had security at the door checking people for weapons. They collected guns and knives and all kinds of weapons. Virtually everybody who came in had a weapon. Everybody had an opinion. Most of the population was anti-defendants, *and* anti-the-attorneys from out of town. Outside attorneys seldom are welcomed in the smaller towns out in the state. And the same went for Lawrence who was with them, to watch Frank's back.

Frank, Big Frank and Lawrence had talked about it. But Big Frank did not want his son going to this town. Lawrence would travel with Frank anyway, since he was a bondsman, and the two of them were acutely aware of narrow attitudes in different towns. Lawrence knew it would be dangerous for Frank to represent these people down there, so his sole purpose was to watch Frank's back.

On the very first day of trial, the girl showed up in a leopard-skin dress, heavy make-up, beehive hairdo, short dress, black mesh stockings, and high heels! Frank Haddad was not a happy camper. He told Lawrence to take his trench coat off, put it on the girl, and button it. The girl was little, and the coat hung practically to the floor. Frank ordered the mother to take her to the restroom to wash her face, and brush her hair out. He gave the mother a rubber band from his briefcase. "Put her hair in a ponytail." Then he told the kid, in a stern voice, "Do not look at the other table."

The girl was devastated. The mother and father were doing everything they could to save their daughter. She was being tried for murder. She was their daughter, and they loved her.

At the first court recess, Frank ordered this mother, "Get a gingham or calico print dress with a Peter-Pan collar, and little satin ribbons." That's how the girl dressed for the remainder of the trial.

So the trial began. There was a lot of publicity. The people in the town did not accept Lawrence and Frank. They were outsiders, and they called their wives every night and gave a report, to let them know they were okay.

Before Lawrence and Frank would call every night, Frank's wife JoAnn would hear from Big Frank, Frank's father. Big Frank was a gruff man, who was pretty much all bark and no bite. But he was gruff and very complaining a lot of times. He had somewhat of a negative attitude about some things. He would say to JoAnn, "They're not coming out alive. They're going to get murdered. We're never going to see my son again. They hate 'em down there!"

He would say things like that to JoAnn. Then JoAnn would call me. She would get upset, very upset. We would try to give one another support. "Yes, they *will* come out alive." We gave one another support. Then Frank would call JoAnn, and Lawrence would call me.

When they would call, Lawrence would have to say, "Hold on! Hold on! Wait just a second!"

A truck would go by on the highway out in front of this motel, and you could actually hear it. The walls shook. You could not carry on a conversation. "Varooooom, boom, boom!"

And then you'd ask, "Okay, now what were you saying?"

They called and checked with us every night. Then JoAnn and I would get together again and say, "Yeah, they're alright. They're going to be okay."

The people of Greenville did not accept these men from out of town. They did not like them at all. Every day in the courtroom the sheriff stood against the wall by a door. He was a big man and the leader of the pack. He made a great effort to glare and stare at Lawrence. Of course, everybody really disliked Mr. Haddad. Frank was wheeling and dealing and swinging into action with the case.

Lawrence never said a thing. He stood mainly at the back of the courtroom, or near the front, depending where he thought was the best position. He would just quietly stand there. After about the second or third day, the sheriff walked up to Lawrence and said, "Who are you?"

"Lawrence Detroy."

"What is your purpose here?"

"My purpose?"

"Are you a lawyer?" asked the sheriff.

"No. I'm no lawyer."

"Well, what is your purpose here?"

"My purpose?" Lawrence pointed to Frank. "There's my friend. I'm watching his back."

The sheriff kind of looked at Lawrence. He said, "What do you mean?"

"I am Frank Haddad's lifelong friend. And I've come down here to make sure no one hurts him. Do you know what 'friends' means? Do you know what 'friendship' is?" Of course, even if you're a bigot, you generally do appreciate friendship.

And this guy said, "Yeah, I know what you mean." He kind of stood back and looked at Lawrence some more.

Frank had to argue some motion or some point of law in the judge's chambers. The court called a recess so Frank and all of the other lawyers could go back to the judge's chambers and do their thing. The sheriff approached Lawrence and said, "Come with me."

So Lawrence felt he was either going to be hurt or not hurt. He didn't know which. The sheriff led him down into the basement of the courthouse. It was a big, old building set in the middle of town. They went down a hallway in the basement. Lawrence said, "I felt I was either being set up, or things were going to be alright."

The sheriff took his keys and unlocked a heavy door. He opened the door onto a room full of confiscated whiskey. He said, "Do you drink?"

Well, Lawrence did drink. And he said, "Oh yeah, I like a drink."

"You know, this is a dry county — you can't get a drink here."

"Yeah, that's right."

"Come on in here."

The whole time Lawrence is feeling he's going to be either hurt or not hurt. He's not sure. But instinctively, he kind of liked this guy, so he went into the room. The sheriff picked up a bottle of whiskey.

Lawrence never was a whiskey drinker — never. He drank Scotch, but he did not like whiskey. But, with these kinds of people, a sign of manhood is to be able to take a good swig of whiskey.

The sheriff handed a bottle to Lawrence. "Do you like this? This is my favorite."

Lawrence says, "Oh man, I love that!"

He takes the bottle and took the cap off. "What do I have to lose?" he thought. He took a great big drink of this whiskey, and it about killed him. Lawrence had a sensitive stomach. Inside, he's like, "Oh, God," but he pretended he really enjoyed it.

"Damn, you drank a lot!"

"Oh man, I needed a drink."

So the guy takes a drink of the whiskey, a substantial swig. Then Lawrence said, "Well, is that it?" He took the bottle back from the guy. The guy's getting ready to put the cap on. Lawrence took another swig. "If I'm gonna go, I'm gonna go tuned up!" he thought.

The sheriff instantly liked Lawrence. So he said, "Well, here." He took a couple of bottles of confiscated whiskey, and Lawrence managed to hedge and get some Scotch. They put it in their pockets and went back upstairs.

During this time, Frank was in the judge's chambers. When he came out, there was Lawrence — tuned. You could always tell when Lawrence was tuned! His eyes would get more blue. Frank asked, "What in the hell is going on?" But he was busy representing his client.

So they go on with the trial, and Lawrence never really knew whether the sheriff was his enemy or friend. It was hard to tell. Frank had to go argue some more motions in the judge's chambers, and Lawrence said to Frank, "Dad, I'll go across the street to that little coffee place and get us a cup of coffee to go."

"Okay, Fox. I'll see you back here."

Lawrence leaves and the courthouse empties. Everybody leaves, because there's another recess. Lawrence goes over to this little restaurant. It's an old place with booths. The whole community is in there. You've got farmers in their overalls. Everybody's discussing the case. They're all talking about it. Lawrence goes up to the counter and he says, "Young lady, I'd like a couple cups of coffee, please."

One of the farmers said, "Well, I think they oughta take that little Jew lawyer and tar-and-feather him, and that other guy, and run 'em out of town."

Lawrence felt they said that deliberately for his benefit, because he was there, so he said, "Change that order to a Coke in a bottle and leave the cap on." He thought he was going to have to fight his way out of the restaurant.

In walks the sheriff of the confiscated whiskey. He overhears this conversation, and he hears Lawrence order the bottle of Coke. The sheriff knew what was going on. He said, "I have something I want to tell everybody here." He got their attention. "This man is a friend of that lawyer that's across the street. And we all know what friends are." He said, "Nobody will hurt this man or that lawyer." He paused. "I like them."

From that time on, they were accepted in Greenville. Poor Aubrey Williams had a horrible time. Horrible. He had to try to collect a fee from the defendants' families, and they lived back in an inaccessible marsh. He had a horrible, horrible time getting to them. There was no road. He might have gotten a chicken or something.

But when they concluded that trial, Frank walked the girl, and the two men were sent to the penitentiary.

When they came to Louisville, they had a trunk full of hams, casseroles, pies, and everything. The community turned out to be very nice to Lawrence and Frank. But in the beginning we were quite frightened. We thought for sure they were going to get hurt, and, honestly, they did too.

Senator Cook Waits

Marlowe Cook was a United States Senator, and he and Lawrence and Frank were real good friends. When he would come to town, he would have lunch with them. This was in the days when Lawrence was wheeling and dealing and constantly in the center of things. He picked Marlowe up at the airport and they went to Frank's office. They're waiting patiently in the reception area for Frank to finish with a client.

Marlowe's got the big head. He's the United States Senator, and he's suddenly ticked off. Lawrence is laughing at him. He thinks it's funny. Marlowe said, "Well, I don't understand it. I'm a United States Senator. I can't believe I'm being kept waiting out here."

Lawrence said, "Well, there's the door! Go on and go eat lunch by yourself." Lawrence had no airs.

Cook's sitting there grumbling and carrying on. Frank finishes with his client. The door opens. Frank steps out. "Fellows, I'll be right with you. I've got one little thing to do." At that moment, the elevator door opens and two people walk in through the open door.

There's this little lady. She's obviously pitifully poor, with her big country bumpkin son. The woman had no teeth. Both were straggly. They were just dirt poor, and ignorant, from down in the country. She said, "I've got to see that Mr. Haddad! I gotta see Frank Haddad. I've come to see him."

The receptionist said, "I'm sorry…. Do you have an appointment? What's your name?"

"I don't have an appointment. My son's in trouble, they're trying to railroad him, I've come to the best lawyer I know of. It's Frank Haddad, and I want him to represent my son."

"Well now, Ma'am, you have to have an appointment."

Frank steps out and hears this woman giving this spiel to the receptionist. So he said, "Come right in my office."

So he takes the woman and the boy, who's being charged with murder, into his office.

They were really, really ragpickers. They were pitifully poor. They were in with Frank. Marlowe is livid. "Can you believe that? We are going out to lunch. I am a United States Senator!" He is having a fit because when you are a Senator, you should be treated like a superstar.

Frank's in with them for twenty minutes. Then he brings them out. He pitches them to another lawyer in the office to get the information and take care of the details. Marlowe is going to bawl Frank out. Lawrence is laughing, because he thinks it's funny.

Senator Cook says, "Mr. Haddad, I can't believe you would make me wait for those people."

Frank said, "Let me explain something to you, Marlowe. You not only waited for those people...."

"You're not going to fool with those people, are you?"

"I'm going represent them. That woman's son is sure to get railroaded if I don't. I'm going to represent him, and you're going to pay for it!"

Marlowe was stunned. But he got over it. And he *did* pay for it. And Frank walked the boy.

Whatever he was charged with, a murder down in the state, in the country somewhere, he was being railroaded because they were ignorant, and they didn't know what they were doing. But the woman was smart. There's a lot to be said for people with education, and people with street smarts. She was smart enough to skip over all those country bumpkin lawyers and come straight to the city, dragging her poor, ignorant son with her, and get the best lawyer in Kentucky.

That was Frank and Lawrence. Marlowe had his comeuppance. From that point on, they used to laugh about it. They would tease him about it. They'd say, "Remember when you had the big head, Marlowe?"

He'd say, "Man, I had to pay a hell of a price." Because he had to pay for the case, along with some others.

FRIENDS

In the relationship of the two couples, there was constant laughter. We laughed and needled and cajoled and teased each other. We found little things to set the others up. As couples, we understood each other and accepted that and loved it. The other thing was our loyalty to one other. JoAnn and Frank always knew that we would be 100% loyal to them as they were loyal to us. It was a neat thing to have friends like that.

Sebastiani Winery

The four of us went to San Francisco when Lawrence was a member of the liquor dealers' association. They had planned with a winery to give us a tour, but JoAnn and I were not interested. Lawrence said, "Well, this is business," meaning we should go on this tour of the Sebastiani winery. These people had prearranged this, and it was supposed to be pretty important.

So we go to Las Vegas and we have a good time. Then we go to San Francisco. All this time we're eating, we're drinking, we're shopping, we're getting in trouble, we're having a good time. The least thing we wanted to do was tour a winery. It's like pulling our nails out. So, JoAnn and I proceeded to whine about it a couple of days ahead of time.

We get to San Francisco, and Lawrence said, "Well, we're here for four days, so we've got to go to the Sebastiani winery because these people have gone to the trouble."

"Oh, do we have to go? We don't want to go." We were really whining about it.

Frank said, "Beverly, we've got to go. JoAnn, both of y'all, settle down. You have to go, because they know there's husbands and wives."

So we rent a car, and the car was horrible. It was some little midget car, and Lawrence was six-foot-whatever big. And Frank was big. This car was little and had a console in the front seat. It was a miserable car. It was spring, but it was burning up heat in San Francisco, and JoAnn and I had hangovers from the day before. I mean we were really not feeling right, so we complained all through breakfast. We complained the night before, and we complained all through breakfast. We did not want to go to this winery. Beefed about it, but to no avail.

The men had made up their minds, and we were stuck. So we get in the car, and we're in the back seat. The men were in the front seat. JoAnn's going, "I don't know why we have to go. I don't know. I don't understand why we have to go. We could have stayed at the hotel. We could have slept in."

Lawrence is being very patient. Lawrence was a very patient man. But Frank would get mad, and he told us to shut up. The more he told us to shut up, the louder we'd beef. The winery is eighty miles away. We're riding in this hot sun, and the car is miserable. We're feeling really bad, and the roads are winding. We're driving along the ocean thinking, "Oh, God, if we ever get to this place...."

Our deal was, we'd get in and we'd get out. We'd make a showing. We'd say, "Thank you, we appreciate it," then we're gone. That's what we planned.

So we drive up to the place.

It had a beautiful gate and elegant this and elegant that. We drove up and this gorgeous gate was all wrought iron. It was unbelievably beautiful. Creek stone fences, and the gate's open, and there's a guard out there. JoAnn and I are in the back seat. We're still whining. I said, "Well, it's a pretty place."

She goes, "Yeah, it is pretty."

We drive up to this absolutely stunning house. It's a Falcon Crest type place. The guard told us the son-in-law of the man who owned this winery would be taking us on this tour. They were waiting on us. We were going, "Ohhhh!" We were still whining.

Then the guy comes out. I swear to God, he looked like Tom Selleck. He was *so* handsome. He was better than Tom Selleck. He was so very handsome. JoAnn goes, "Well!"

I go, "Well!" We suddenly got really interested in the winery.

Frank picks up on it immediately. The guy introduces himself. I think his name was Woodford. He said, "I'm So-and-so."

And we went, "Oh, oh, my goodness," and "Oh, I'm so excited!" We changed our attitude 100%, a three-hundred-and-sixty-degree turn. We were real enthusiastic. And Frank got mad at us because he picked up on that.

And so when we went into the winery, this guy's taking us through. He's telling us stuff about big, giant pieces of equipment and JoAnn and I were beside ourselves. "Oh, it's really nice equipment!" Everything he told us, we asked him to repeat. I'd say, "Now, what did you say that thing does there?" And he'd answer, and I'd say, "Oh, that's fascinating!"

We feigned interest in this wine equipment which, honest to God, we couldn't have cared less about. We were milking it for all we could because this guy was so handsome. He got flattered. These two women were *very* flattering. The whole time we're talking, my husband, Lawrence, is being cool. He knows we're all show and no go. But Frank is testy. He's standing behind the man and he's going like this, like he's spiteful, as if to say, "You knock it off."

The guy would say something about a red grape, and I'd say, "Is it red-red or is it purple-red?" We stretched everything out. The guy's ego got real big, because he'd never had people show so much interest in the winery. Our interest was really superficial. We were only after the man's body.

He announces, "You know, I was given permission to spend all day with you all."

Frank says, "It's not necessary."

I said, "Oh, yes it is!"

JoAnn says, "Oh, absolutely!"

So he said, "You know what, let me make a phone call. I'll make arrangements to take you all out to lunch."

But Frank says, "Oh, that's okay. You don't have to go to all that trouble."

We said "Okay." And we accepted the invitation. The guy ran to make his phone call to clear it with his people. Frank is furious.

He said, "What the hell are you two doing? What do you think you're doing?"

"Nothing! You wanted us to show interest in the winery. We're showing interest in the winery!"

"I know what the hell you all are doing. You're flirting with that guy."

I said, "We are not! How can you say such a thing?"

Lawrence, the peacemaker, said, "Dad, the girls are interested in the winery! Just let 'em enjoy it." Lawrence was so cool.

Lawrence was not drinking at that time, but Frank was. Sometimes he would have a drink and sometimes he wouldn't. Our host takes us to a Mexican restaurant. It was the oldest Mexican restaurant, it was the original Mexican restaurant, in California.

At that time I had never eaten Mexican food. He said, "Do you like Mexican food?"

I said, "I love it!"

JoAnn said, "You don't even like Mexican food. You've never eaten Mexican food!"

I said, "If that guy says he's Mexican, I'm eating Mexican!"

We go to this place, and they knew this guy. Then he says there are specific wines that go really good with Mexican food. We said, "Well by all means. We honor the Sebastiani winery because, after all, you're giving us the tour." We milked it for all we could.

We sit there and have this wonderful wine. There was a wine you had *before* the Mexican food, there was a wine you had *with* the Mexican food, and there was a wine you had *after* the Mexican food. Frank and Lawrence were not drinking anything. Frank was at the end of the table.

As time went on, this guy told us everything. He was really a nice fellow. He was having a ball because he had two women totally interested in him. We're giggling, we're laughing, and everything.

We head back to the winery. When we get in the car, this guy's real big. He's still Tom Selleck. He's real, real big. Six-foot-four or five. We wanted him to get in the back with us. So I get in the car, and I scoot all the way over against the side. I'm riding sidesaddle. And JoAnn scoots all the way in. We've got plenty of room for this man in the back seat.

Frank flips the seat back and says, "You're riding up front with us," and made the guy ride the console! Frank was really mean to him.

Now we know we're in trouble because Frank didn't appreciate us flirting. But Lawrence was being a sport. He was being real polite and nice.

When we get back to the winery, this guy says, "You know, I was told I could spend all day long with you."

Frank says, "It's enough."

"We've done enough," our host replied. "But we very rarely take anyone into our boardroom where we do our winetasting."

JoAnn and I immediately said, "Okay! Let's go!" We were ready.

Frank said, "It's not necessary. We don't really need to see it."

I said, "Oh, yes, we do, Mr. Haddad! Mr. Detroy is in the liquor business, and I need to see it." I raised hell with him about it.

So we went upstairs. It was an absolutely gorgeous room. The door was a great big, giant door with hand-carved grape clusters and leaves. The boardroom had big, enormous, long, gorgeous tables of wood, with big, high-backed chairs with grape clusters. The winery collected wooden ducks and mallards.

I asked, "What is that particular breed of duck?" He had mallards all around his boardroom. There must have been 200 of them. I made him tell us what every one was. Frank was getting furious. He was so mad.

"Oh, this is such-and-such a duck. This is such-and-such a mallard." We really didn't want to know, but we dragged it out.

He proceeds to bring the wine. "This is how we do a wine tasting." He set the wine out. They had these tiny little glasses, which were wine glasses, but they were miniatures. You're supposed to take it and sip it and spit it out.

JoAnn said, "I'm not going to do that. Spitting out's gross." I said, "I guarantee you, I'm going to drink it!"

We got in so much trouble. The guy got tuned up. We got tuned up. Frank had had it. He crossed his arms in front of his chest. He was so furious at us. Finally, he stood up and said, "Let's go!" real sharp. He was so huffy.

So we left. As we were getting in the car, I said, "JoAnn, we're really in trouble."

She said, "I know it. We are really." Frank was furious at us.

But the guy loved us. He hugged us. We wallowed in that. "Ooh!" We liked that. We gave him our address and told him to call us anytime he was in Louisville. We were bad. I know we were bad.

We get in the car. JoAnn and I were sitting in the back. She said, "Frank's going to kill us."

"No. He's your husband; he's going to kill you. *My* husband is understanding, and he knows I'm just signifying and joking. You're the one who's in trouble."

Then we started giggling. She said, "Don't laugh. Frank will get mad. We're supposed to be scared. Frank'll get mad if he thinks we're not scared."

When he got in the car, he started hollering. He bawled us out to beat the band. Lawrence was saying, "Well, Dad, the girls are just havin' a good time."

Then the next thing you know we both passed out cold in the back seat. That was it. Frank looked around and there we were — one facing one way and the other facing the other way. JoAnn's head on one window, my head on the other. We were out cold.

SAN FRANCISCO TROLLEY RIDE

On this San Francisco trip, Lawrence and JoAnn and I loved to walk and window shop, and go in stores. We loved to visit different areas, and talk to people and mingle, and get the flavor of the community or the place we were in. We loved that. But Frank hated that. That was sheer torture for Frank. Frank would walk into a store and say, "Uh-huh. I've seen it before."

This didn't interest Frank Haddad at all. It was sheer torture. Plus, Frank complained about his feet hurting. He never wanted to admit his weight caused his feet to hurt. He always claimed that JoAnn and I and Lawrence ruined his feet, because we made him walk all over Chinatown to look in these stores he couldn't have cared less about. Shopping did not impress Frank Haddad.

We badgered Frank. We said things like, "We want to go here," or "We want to go there."

Frank protested, "I don't want to see that. I don't want to do that." But we badgered him. One day we decided we wanted to ride a trolley car. Frank was adamant that he didn't want to do that. "That's stupid. Everybody does that — dumb, dumb." It started at breakfast. He said, "I don't want to go. It's just tourist stuff. I don't want to get on that. I see no fascination whatsoever getting on a trolley car." We're sitting there, JoAnn and I, and then Lawrence chimed in with us. We're whining that we wanted to do that. We were in San Francisco, and we wanted to ride on a trolley car. Then we started accusing Frank of being a poophead. He was just a dullard. He wasn't any fun. We went on and on and on. We just absolutely demoralized poor Frank Haddad. He was really a stick-in-the-mud because he wouldn't do these things we wanted to do. After all, there were four of us, and three wanted to do something. He was only one, so it was three against one. And finally we badgered Frank into going on this trolley car.

But Frank let it be known that he was going under duress. He raised hell. "You all dragged me through all this tourist stuff." He's just furious at us. We're laughing, because we know we've got him where we want him. We didn't show him any respect.

A trolley car comes up. There was a tremendous amount of tourists and people around. But we get on the trolley car. And Lawrence and JoAnn and I get on one side of the trolley car. There wasn't room there for a fourth, which would have been Frank. So Frank gets directly across from where we're sitting. And we're sitting right by the railing that is like a divider. It was a brass railing. That's where Frank sat, right next to this divider railing. He was directly across from us.

Behind him, a woman gets on the trolley car. She had to weigh at least 250-plus pounds. She was short and fat. She was exactly as wide as she was tall. She had enormous arms that had this enormous amount of fat hanging off of them. She had shopping bags and packages, like you would not believe. She was just loaded down. Her hands and arms were full of all of these packages. The woman made grunting sounds because she was fat and heavy and couldn't maneuver, and this was a crowded trolley car, and she grunted as she tried to squeeze past people. People were literally falling backwards to get out of her way to let her through. She was so big.

So we're sitting there. The three of us are sitting on one side, and Frank's on the other side. And we're laughing and giggling because we know we won; we got on the trolley car and we overruled Frank. The three of us know we've won. Frank has not surrendered. He's going along with it. But he's still a little miffed at the three of us.

This woman waddles over and decides to sit next to Frank. I'll always remember that day. Frank sat there. This woman squeezed in. There was a young girl on one side of her, and Frank on the other. The girl literally just about fell off the bench. The bench should have held five people, but when this woman sat down, it was lucky to hold the three of them.

She squeezed poor Frank up against this brass railing, until his arms were going all the way up holding on to the railing. It was all he could do to even stay in the seat. She squished in there. Then the poor girl almost fell off the other side of the bench.

The woman settles in, with all her packages. She's like a bird settling in on its nest. She wiggles until she gets herself situated just exactly right. Frank isn't real happy. We're looking at this, and we're laughing, because we know how miserable poor Frank is. But we're not miserable. We're comfortable. We're sitting together, and we have plenty of room. We're in a real good position, and we get to watch poor Frank in his misery.

The trolley car would go up a hill, and there would be no problem. But when it would go down those steep hills of San Francisco, which is a straight shot down, this woman would roll, literally, all over poor Frank. She had her arms around these packages. Her big arms with all that fat hanging down from them would roll right into poor Frank's face and smash him up against the railing.

By the time we got to where we were going, Mr. Haddad was not a happy camper. We never got on another trolley car in San Francisco.

CHINATOWN FIGHT

Lawrence loved to buy gifts for JoAnn. JoAnn was his buddy. He adored JoAnn. He loved to start collections of things for her. He thoroughly enjoyed shopping for a gift for JoAnn.

Years ago, he had started a collection of Canton Rose oriental dishware for JoAnn. This particular style of china was hand-painted. It was Oriental china in pink and blue shades with scenes of people on it. It is really pretty china. You used to be able to buy it at Stewart's.

It became more and more difficult to find this particular style because it had stopped being produced. But you could, on rare occasions, find a piece of this china. When you did, you'd get real excited. Lawrence and I had given JoAnn cups and saucers and a teapot, a tea set, of this china, but she broke one of the cups.

So we decided to go to Chinatown. But Frank didn't want to go to Chinatown. He put up a beef about it. He did not want to go. "I'm not going to damn Chinatown! It's stupid!"

Lawrence was the peacemaker. He would always say, "But Dad, the girls want to go shopping. Let's go to Chinatown."

So we went to Chinatown. And it was total duress on Frank's part. He hated it. He despised it. The whole time he grumbled, he griped, he complained, and we just ignored him. We didn't care, because we were getting what we wanted.

Chinatown in San Francisco is very busy. We were going from place to place, shopping.

Lawrence entertained Frank out on the street. Lawrence bought a basket of shrimps that he offered to Frank. "Here, Dad, take a piece." He'd feed him down the row of stores. Or they'd stand outside a store and girlwatch. Lawrence's job was to keep Frank busy while JoAnn and I went into the store and did our thing.

We weren't supposed to know they were girlwatching. Of course, Frank loved a pretty woman. He liked to look at pretty women.

We went in stores, and we looked at silks and at different, beautiful jewelry, and a thousand things. We just thoroughly enjoyed it.

Most of these little stores were family-owned stores. The great-grandchildren, the grandchildren, the parents, and the grandparents ran these little stores. It was all family-operated. There was a definite, observable hierarchy. The elderly people, the oldest, were the most respected.

We go into this one little store. In the window, we see the perfect Canton Rose teacup and saucer to match JoAnn's broken cup. She got all excited. She said, "Oh, my gosh! There's that cup! Oh, my gosh. I can get my set complete again!"

So we went into the store. There was this little, bitty, tiny lady. She must have been 200 years old — this little Oriental lady with her hair pulled back in a severe bun. The woman wasn't four feet tall. A little, tiny thing. She was the matriarch of this family. She wore a black dress and heavy black walking shoes. Young people were there, but they asked the woman to make decisions. They asked her, and she would okay it or not okay it. She controlled this store.

JoAnn goes and gets this cup and saucer. She picks it up and tells the lady she just wants to buy the cup. This upset the little Oriental lady tremendously. She became absolutely livid at JoAnn and started yelling at her. She said, "What?! You mean you buy cup without saucer? Who ever heard of anyone buy cup without saucer? I never heard of such a thing." She went on this tangent.

I thought, "Oh my God...." She absolutely got plum violent at JoAnn. And JoAnn, being stubborn, and having the Italian temper that *she's* got, got mad, too.

She said, "Well, all I want is the cup. I don't need the saucer. I have a saucer. I want the cup. That's all I want to buy. Just split the set."

These two women get into an argument. I'm thinking, "Well, we're going to get whipped in Chinatown. It's going to be a 200-year-old, four-foot woman, who's going to whip JoAnn. Then I go out on the street and signal Lawrence we're having trouble. "Lawrence, I need your help." I explained, "The Oriental lady's going to whip JoAnn. It's the Italians against the Orient!"

So Lawrence walks in. Here are these two women arguing over JoAnn's nerve wanting to buy just a cup, and the woman shouting, "What you mean buy cup without saucer? Whoever heard of buy cup without saucer?" She screamed, "You take extra saucer and you use for fortune cookies!"

When Lawrence comes in, JoAnn is swinging mad. She gets huffy, and she's hot. She doesn't like being told she can't do something when she sees no reason why there's a problem. But this little lady feels deeply and can't see how's she going to sell a saucer without a cup. But JoAnn's goal was to just replace this one little piece.

Frank said, "My God, if we get out of this place alive, it'll be a miracle!"

Now Lawrence, the peacemaker, is in the store. He says, "Alright, lady, I'll take the saucer. She'll take the cup." So then we settled the fight.

When we got out of that store, Frank said, "It's great." We all thought it would be the "Fight in Chinatown," but at the end, JoAnn got the cup and we got the saucer. JoAnn uses that saucer for fortune cookies.

Piña Colada

One time we were in Las Vegas. Lawrence and Frank knew a lot of people in Vegas. They knew casino operators and gamblers. Lawrence and Frank had stayed in contact with people from Louisville who had moved to Las Vegas. When they would visit these individuals, JoAnn and I would kill time.

One day the guys were going to the Horseshoe or some place downtown to visit the Purple Man. He was a friend of Lawrence's. We always called him Purple Man.

Purple Man was a character who always wore shades of purple. He would wear purple silk shirts and gabardine slacks. He had leather shoes. They were really pretty shades of purple, and the man had snow-white hair and a beautiful tan. I never understood what Purple Man did. I think he was a gambler and bookmaker. I'm not exactly sure what. But he had a long-running relationship with Lawrence and Frank.

Purple Man was a sweet man, a soft-spoken man. He would send Lawrence and me letters with Vegas newspaper clippings of articles he thought we'd be interested in. Lawrence would share these clippings with Frank. The articles were about this casino or that casino, or different individuals Lawrence and Frank knew out there, and whatever was going on. Purple Man's letters were written with purple ink. He was an unusual man.

Purple Man had taken Lawrence and Frank to some place where they were going to gamble this day. So JoAnn and I decided to stay at the hotel and go swimming.

Neither one of us know, really, how to swim. Plus, I'm very, very, very fair-complected, and the sun absolutely kills me. But I decide I can handle it. So we went to this hotel swimming pool. We rented a couple of rafts. They were big, fancy things with arm rests on them. Neither one of us could get on them.

The pool had a lot of people around it, a lot of conventioneers, which was typical of Las Vegas. We get into this pool, and we finally manage to get on our rafts. She and I both have a fear of drowning, so we're careful to float in the shallow end of the pool. But there are so many people around. You're on a raft. The raft tends to float. You fall asleep. The sun is so hot in Vegas. You fall asleep on the raft. The next thing you know, you're about ready to go over the line.

JoAnn kept floating her raft over the line. There was a conventioneer there who had a bald head. I remember. His head was so shiny with the sun shining down. He would jump in the water and swim, and his head would be wet. It was just *blinding*, this man's bald head.

He was somewhat of a flirt, and a conventioneer, and he sees these two women by themselves. I have no idea what his impression of us was, but anyway we behaved like we always do. We always seem to get in trouble or attract trouble. We're laughing and having a good time. There's something about people having a good time that attracts other people. It never fails. Wherever we are, JoAnn and I always attract other people around us.

We're in the pool. She keeps bumping into this bald-headed guy. The guy starts flirting with JoAnn. JoAnn is not really paying a heck of a lot of attention. Her main goal is trying to keep from drowning.

It's so hot. There's a cocktail waitress walking around the apron of the pool. She's carrying a tray of frozen drinks that look absolutely wonderful. We're sitting there in the hot sun, and it's over a hundred degrees. We're parched and we see these snow-white, frozen, frosted drinks. They look glorious. JoAnn said, "Let's get a couple of those drinks."

I said, "Oh yeah, sounds good to me!"

We're really not drinkers. We like an occasional wine. But as far as really drinking, JoAnn and I are not really drinkers. We order a couple of these frozen drinks. They were piña coladas. We go and stake out a spot on the side of the pool. We get rid of one of the rafts, and we take the other raft and put it across the front of us and we sit on the steps that lead down into the pool. We use the raft as a table.

We ordered these piña coladas and we sat there. We drank those piña coladas like they were milkshakes. They were just so delicious, and we're not thinking in terms of the liquor that's in a piña colada. We're thinking in terms of how good it tastes. It was so refreshing, so cold, so wonderful. We knocked out piña coladas.

Then we order a couple more. We're sitting there, and people were coming up and talking to us. We were telling stories. We were laughing. Before long, we have a crowd gathered around us and we both are getting mellow. We're drinking these drinks. The sun's beating down. We're drinking these frozen drinks like they're lemonade. We don't realize they are *not* lemonade. There's rum in these drinks. Rum and hot sun, especially when you're dehydrated and not thinking that way.

We're telling these stories and laughing and joking. Meanwhile, the guys come back from their day of gambling. They had had a particularly good day. They knew we'd be at the pool. Frank said when he walked through the door out to the pool area, he saw an enormous crowd, and he knew in his heart that, in the center of this crowd, were JoAnn and Beverly.

He walked up. Sure enough, we're sitting on the steps. All these people have gathered around us. We're telling stories. We're laughing and giggling. Everybody is using our little raft as a cocktail table. We are just plum looped. Both of us.

Frank looked at us both. We looked up and saw Lawrence and Frank both standing there. Frank had his hands on his hips, and he was real firm. He said, "OUT! Both of you! *Out, right now!*"

And we, oh my God, we flew! We got up out of that pool. I don't even know how we got back to the rooms. The next day, I was so sunburned I could not move. I had a white linen dress I was going to wear to dinner, but I could not wear linen at all. It was too rough. My skin was just parched.

But we did have a good time. I really like piña coladas. I just haven't had any since.

The Glass of Wine

The four of us went to Las Vegas first and then to San Francisco. Las Vegas was an exciting town, but JoAnn and I don't gamble, and we aren't quick enough to understand the intricacies of betting and gambling. We endured Las Vegas in order to get to San Francisco. We loved San Francisco.

We went to Ghirardelli Square and Chinatown every day. We went to the Fairmont. We stayed at beautiful places and traveled to many neat spots. This was the trip when we toured the Sebastiani winery.

One evening we learned Al Martino, the singer, would be entertaining at a dinner supper at the Fairmont hotel. The Fairmont is an old, beautiful hotel in San Francisco. The Fairmont was just a beautiful place with old-style service. It was elegant. We went there that evening.

On this trip, we took turns picking up the tab. One night, it would be our turn to pick up the tab. The next night it would be Frank's turn. And we'd switch back and forth. This was Frank's night out.

We go to the Fairmont. We get a table in a room with a stage. The entertainer was standing down. The small stage wasn't up very high. He was pretty much on our level, with the customers. It was a very intimate atmosphere. We went first class with the meals. The Fairmont had crystal and silver, lovely bone china, and linen tablecloths. It was just beautiful. Candlelit and elegant. The old, patterned carpet was plush and gorgeous. Everything about the evening was beautiful.

Our waiter's an older gentleman. He'd obviously been a waiter there for many years. The maître d' seated us at a really nice table. It was a circular table. Frank loved to order wine. He liked wine. He liked to study wine. He analyzed the wine menu and ordered a bottle of wine. The waiter was very proper and perfect, just perfect.

He takes the order and brings out crystal wine glasses. He pours a taste for Frank to check it out. Frank smelled it the way you're supposed to. He took the cork and then tasted the wine. It was just perfect. Everything was exactly in line with what anyone would want for a perfect evening.

We sat and began our dinner. Al Martino didn't start singing immediately. We had the first course of dinner, and then the singer was to come out. A band was playing music. It was old-fashioned dance music. It was a nice atmosphere. We're sitting laughing and telling stories, and finally Al Martino comes out. He started singing. His voice was mellow and soft. He sang old standards.

The waiter who was waiting on us kept removing our wine glasses. I would have half of a glass of wine, but yet he would remove it and come back with a fresh glass. I had noticed it earlier. I thought, "Why does he keep doing that?" but I was paying attention to the singer. I wondered why he was doing that.

I watched him walk through the swinging doors into the kitchen. He hesitated, then he took one of our glasses off the tray, and he took a big swig! I thought, "I can't believe it. That guy's drinking our wine!"

We didn't want to stir up anything, so we went on watching the entertainer. The entertainer started singing an old standard love song. The waiter comes out. He had brought us another round of fresh glasses and poured more wine for us. By this time, he's tuned up.

Our chairs were turned sideways so we could observe the singer. The waiter goes behind JoAnn's chair, and he puts his arm on the back of JoAnn's chair. He stands there as though he's with JoAnn and they're a couple! Frank is sitting at the table, and he's staring at this waiter. We're a little taken back by this. The singer is singing this song. JoAnn's attention is completely absorbed in the singer. She isn't the least bit aware the waiter is standing there with his arm on the back of her chair.

Al Martino started singing this standard old ballad, a love song, and the waiter looks at JoAnn and says, "That's my favorite!"

JoAnn said, "Oh it's mine, too." And you would have thought they were together! It was like they were the couple. I started giggling.

Frank was mad. He's like, "That's my *wife*." "That's my wife," he said.

Through the rest of the evening, it didn't matter what we needed at our table. Neither myself, nor Lawrence, nor Frank could get anything. We couldn't get a second cup of coffee. We couldn't get Sweet'n Low. But if JoAnn even blinked her eye that she needed the least little thing, this waiter would run over to her and get it for her. It was like she was the only person at our table.

As the evening went on, Frank was getting a little bit irritated. The waiter, meanwhile, was getting very tuned. He must have been taking everybody's wine glasses and drinking them.

But the food was wonderful. The service was good until he fell in love with JoAnn. The entertainer was marvelous. The atmosphere was wonderful. But it sort of put a crimp in everyone's style when the waiter moved in with JoAnn.

As we were leaving, Frank paid the bill. It was a big bill, because the Fairmont was expensive. Frank always tipped very generously. And even though he was irritated with the waiter, he saw a lot of humor in this. He was kind of laughing, too, at the situation. We didn't think the waiter was being vicious. He was in love, apparently. Frank gave the waiter a very generous tip. The waiter took the money. It was in a leather folder. He took the money. It was a big tip. It was cash. He looked at JoAnn and just kind of blew her a kiss. He winked at her, and silently whispered, "Thank you."

IV. GANG GOES FISHING

Fishing Gear
"Here's Your Cap, Fox!"
"No Perch in This Lake"
Patoka Lake
"Bev, I'm Going Under!"

Fishing Gear

Lawrence and Frank were hilarious fishermen. It seemed like they were always doing something.

These men could be sold anything if they were told that it would catch them a bass. We used to fish at Lakewood Gardens in LaGrange. It was near Al Horton's nursery for bedding plants. He had three lakes at this place. The fellows would stock the lakes. It was a neat place to go fishing. We went there a lot, usually on Sundays.

These little lakes were very small. They had boats, but the guys never could quite get to where the fish were. This is true with fishermen in general. The fish in that lake are always in a spot that's not here; it's always *over there*. The one place where the fish are always evades the fishermen. But Lawrence and Frank were always trying to get to that spot.

Allied Sporting Goods has this new thing. It's inner tubes. It's sturdier than a regular inner tube, and it had Army canvas on it. There were pockets on the outside of this inner tube to hold lures and gear. They went all around the outside of the inner tube. On the inside, the center of the inner tube was like a seat. You'd step into it. The guys had these. I guess you'd call them trout fisherman pants, or waterproof thingamajiggers that you put on.

The lake was not deep. You could really walk into this lake. It was a nice little lake. Their idea was that they could get to that spot, they could just get right on top of it, and then they could catch the fish. So they bought these two inner tubes and they went out to the lake.

Lawrence was tall. Frank was short. Both were clumsy. They both stepped into the inner tubes. They have all their gear and everything that they're going to need. There was even a spot for a fishing rod. You could attach the pole onto this inner tube. A fisherman could move into one of these inner tubes and live. That was how neat these things were.

Lawrence gets into one, Frank gets into one, and they walk into the water. Everything's going fine. Immediately Lawrence starts casting the line. He's standing there. This is the life. He just knows he's getting to where the fish are.

Frank started casting his line, too. They're walking out into the lake. The only thing is, Frank's short, and Lawrence is tall. Lawrence keeps walking. His feet still touch the bottom. Frank's feet don't reach as far. He starts floating. He has no way of controlling this little inner tube.

Lawrence quietly fishes on. He's concentrating on whatever he's looking out at, while Frank's going, "Fox! Fox! Hey, Fox! Fox!" The breeze starts taking Frank out into the lake.

Lawrence is walking along in his inner tube, and he's going, "Yeah, Dad." He's not looking at Frank. He couldn't care less about Frank. He's interested in getting that fish. That fish they're there to catch.

Before you know it, Lawrence turns around. Frank's not next to him. Frank's drifting out into the middle of the lake with the breeze. His little, short, stubby legs are no help. He's paddling like crazy trying to get back.

He can't get back. He can't control what's happening, because he's just too little. Lawrence patiently walked over and grabbed Frank by the inner tube and pulled him back. That's how they fished. He held onto Frank by holding onto this stupid inner tube.

"Here's Your Cap, Fox!"

Lawrence and Frank were fishing out at Pat Mitchell's place. Ron Hillerich was with them, and Monk Bevin. Ron Hillerich said Frank and Lawrence always had so many accidents fishing.

They were out fishing. Frank was in the front of the boat, and Ron was in the back. Lawrence always wore his steel-rim glasses and wore a cap. He was known for his caps. He had these caps from England that were tweeds. It was a "Lawrence cap." Anybody who knew Lawrence knew he had a cap on. Lawrence was in the middle.

Frank takes his fishing pole. He zips it back. He's going to cast out. When he zips the line back, the lure catches Lawrence's hat. He zips the hat all the way into the lake.

Frank's sitting there. He could see the cap floating on the water. To know Frank was to know how he always stayed on top of a situation. It didn't matter what the situation was, he always made it look smooth, like there was nothing to it. He looks around and says, "Don't worry about it, Fox! I'll get that cap."

Lawrence is not saying much. And Frank casts his line out and snares the cap with his artificial bait, and reels it in. He smoothly reels it in. He's got this attitude of arrogance like, "Well, there was a problem, but I solved it." He was thinking, "It's just so cool, the way I was able to do that."

He takes the cap off the artificial bait, soaking wet. He hands it to Lawrence, and says, "Here's your cap, Fox!"

Lawrence took it and said, "That's nice, Dad. The only thing is, my glasses are out there, too!"

"No Perch in This Lake"

Ron and Gary Hillerich's father's name was Russ Hillerich. Russ was a detective for Frank Haddad. He was a good and dear friend. He was Frank's true fishing partner. Lawrence came later in life as Frank's fishing partner.

Russ encouraged Lawrence and me to go fishing with him. He was going to teach me how to fish. Whenever you fished with these men, they were always loaded with advice. "Do this... Do this... Go here... Go there...." Russ saw this. Russ was a sweet man. He was a patient fishing partner. He decided this day he was going to take me under his wing and teach me how to fish, and let the guys do their fishing. They were going to fish as partners.

So we went to a lake. It was some little farm lake in Indiana. It was on Sam Roy's farm.

We were standing on the bank casting out. Russ said to me, "Don't tell the guys, but I'm going to teach you how to walk a worm. But we won't tell them that's what we're doing."

Of course, I'm a novice. I don't know anything. I said, "Sure. Whatever you want to do, Russ." So he puts a worm on my line, and a weight, so that the line would go down to the bottom of the lake. Then we cast out the line. It goes far out into the lake where it sinks to the bottom.

He said, "Let it sink." When it did, he said, "Reel it back real slow, and bounce the pole up and down, *à la* walk the worm." He knew this was a farm lake. He knew a walking worm would entice more fish than the fancy artificial baits Lawrence and Frank were using.

Lawrence and Frank were standing fifty feet away from where we were. But they were at that famous spot where they were going to catch the fish. And we were *not* at that spot. This is the way fishermen think.

I'm walking the worm, and we're not having much luck. After thirty minutes or so nobody was getting any hits. Frank and Lawrence were getting a little impatient. They wondered if any fish were even in this lake. Russ encourages me to keep walking the worm. I'm doing as he tells me to do. I walked the worm in; I cast the line back out. I walked the worm in, I cast it back out. I'm getting pretty good at doing it.

All of a sudden, I had this real hard hit on my line. Something took my line straight out in the water so hard that it jerked the pole all the way down. I thought, "God! What? Oh, God, what have I got?" At first I thought I had it snagged, because I always was getting things snagged.

It was not a snag. The line was moving. It tore across the lake. Lawrence and Frank hear this sound. It was a distinct sound. Only fishermen really know it. They both came running over. I snap the line back, and I catch whatever is on my line. I start reeling it back.

Frank's saying, "Put the pole up!"

Lawrence is saying, "Put the pole down!"

They're both hollering, "Go! Get this over here! Reel it in! Reel it slow! Go fast!" They're carrying on.

Russ is ever so patient and so sweet. He tells me, "Just do it the way you know how." He gave me quiet guidance, with no yelling and screaming. "Just don't pay any attention to the guys."

I wasn't paying any attention to them. It was *my* fish. I didn't want to listen to their advice. I'm bringing in this fish. I bring it in. It's a beautiful white perch. I mean *beautiful*. It probably weighed three-and-a-half to four pounds, which is a good-sized fish. And perch are neat to catch because they put up a good fight.

Frank, Mr. Know-It-All, says, "There are no perch in this lake."

But I have a perch I'm holding up, and everyone's enthusiastic. Still he said, "There's no perch here."

I said, "But this is a white perch."

"Yeah, but there's no perch in this lake."

"But where did the perch come from, Frank?" I asked. "Did it fall out of the sky? I caught this perch. It was in this lake!"

Although fishermen like to see fellow fishermen catch fish, they want it to be *their* fish, not your fish. The next thing I know, we're taking this fish off the line. We're going to put it in our bucket and save it. Lawrence and Frank are standing in the exact spot that I was just standing in to catch this fish. I get huffy. I said, "Russ, they're standing in my spot! They were standing forty or fifty feet away, and now all of a sudden they're fishing from my spot."

Russ said, "Don't worry about it, Bev. Don't tell them how we got that fish. They think we're using the same type of technique they're using. We'll go over to where they were fishing."

"Okay."

So we packed up our stuff, and we moved over to where the men had been standing in the first place. And they're now where we had been fishing, because apparently, Russ and I had *the* spot. So we go to this other place. Frank and Lawrence are fishing ever more seriously, casting out their artificial baits. We get a worm and throw it out in the lake. I proceed to walk the worm again. I'm getting pretty darn good at this. I'm the world's greatest expert on walking a worm. Russ is laughing. He knows this is the technique that is going to attract the big fish. We've already caught one fish. They're spraying stuff on the baits. I cannot tell all the gear they had. But we've just got a little red worm.

I start walking the worm, and I'll be darned if I didn't get another hit. Out goes the line again. The same identical thing. It was another perch. It was absolutely beautiful. I brought that fish in. Again, the men were screaming and yelling, "Do this! Do that!" But now I'm a professional. I don't need them. I know how to bring in this fish. I've brought one in, and I can bring in another.

I get this fish all the way in. Russ is helping me remove it from the line. Guess where the guys are standing. In the same spot where I just caught this second fish. I surrendered. I gave up. That was it. This is the way fishermen are. They're funny.

The other thing about fishermen that kills me is, there's no such thing as lying. If you're a fisherman, there is no lie. If two men like Lawrence and Frank are fishing partners, and Frank throws out a line and it hits the water, and some little mosquito nibbles on the line, and there's a ripple in the water, Frank would say, "My God! Did you see that hit?!"

Then Lawrence would say, "It looked like a whale to me." It didn't matter.

When they first did this, I said, "Y'all, it was a little ripple in the water!"

"No, it wasn't! It was a big fish, and it got off," they insisted. By the time they'd return home, this hit was so humongous you would have thought it was Moby Dick. I mean, it was so humongous. But this isn't a lie. There's no lies when you're fishing. This has been okayed by God himself, I believe. God was probably a fisherman.

Patoka Lake

Going fishing with Frank and Lawrence was always an adventure. JoAnn and I occasionally went on fishing trips with the fellows, being good wives. We enjoyed it. We enjoyed getting out to some pretty little lake and casting out a line to catch a fish. But JoAnn and I didn't have the serious attitude about fishing that the men had. They breathed fishing and lived fishing, but we did not.

One particular day, we tried out Patoka Lake, a brand new lake in Indiana. It had just been opened. It was exciting for fishermen in this region who could not wait to get into this lake.

We came as we were. Frank Haddad, who forever fought his weight, was on a diet. When Frank was on a diet, he could be the most miserable person to be around: grouchy and bossy and demanding and irritable. That was the frame of mind he was in, although he was still very enthusiastic and thrilled about going to this new lake for fishing.

Lawrence was forever the peacemaker. He always tried to keep things cool and nice. That's what he always said. Somebody would ask, "Lawrence, how are you doing?"

He could be having the most horrible day, and he'd say, "Everything's nice!" That was just the way Lawrence was. He was the peacemaker. He was equally excited as Frank about going to this brand new lake.

JoAnn and I really would have liked to stay in bed. It was like six o'clock in the morning, and we thought, in our opinion, the fish were probably asleep, too. We felt like they needed their good beauty rest like we did. We were up, but we weren't really alert and oriented like we should be. Driving up to this lake early in the morning before the sun had actually risen was not really something that we had tremendous enthusiasm about. But we did it. Under duress, but we did it.

Frank and JoAnn came over to our house. We had a bass boat that Lawrence had attached to the back of the car. They came over. JoAnn and I were fumbling around. My eyes were barely open. The guys were all enthusiastic about their fishing equipment. Frank was bossy and ordering us around. He said, "Get in the car, you two! Come on now, we've gotta go. We've gotta get going."

"Okay, okay." So we get in the car. JoAnn and I get in the back seat. We're grumping between the two of us. "I don't know why we have to go up there this early. This is silly."

Every time we went fishing, this never failed. The minute they opened the trunk to put their boxes of bait and gear in, Lawrence and Frank would proceed to open their boxes and compare their different artificial baits. JoAnn and I would sit in the car and we'd start giggling. It was so silly.

We didn't understand why we had to get up so early in the morning to compare one rubber worm with another rubber worm, or whatever it was they were comparing. "My" little artificial fish with "your" little wooden fish.

It would be the same thing. Frank would say, "Now, Fox, So-and-So said this right here is guaranteed to catch the biggest fish in the lake."

Then Lawrence would tell Frank, "But Dad, So-and-So was down to the Cumberland, and this was what they caught. It was a rainy day." They'd go on and on. Meanwhile, we'd be sitting in the car. JoAnn and I would inevitably start giggling because we'd be summing it up to each other. These two so-called sportsmen, with their agenda to get us up to the lake so early in the morning, were wasting away time standing there doing comparisons of their bait boxes.

But finally, after about ten minutes, they're satisfied with the gear they put in the car. They close the trunk. Then we proceed on. Frank and Lawrence ride up front, and JoAnn and I are in the back.

JoAnn said, "I'm so hungry!" Frank was on a diet and he was not happy to hear her say that.

Frank said, "JoAnn, we're not going to eat anything."

"But, Frank, I'd really like to have a doughnut or something."

"Yeah, Frank — me, too!" I said. "I'd love to have a doughnut!"

"No! No doughnuts!" He got real huffy with us. Huffy to JoAnn and me didn't really mean a whole lot. It was water off our backs. We didn't pay a whole lot of attention.

Lawrence says, "Well, Dad, the girls are hungry. Maybe we can stop somewhere and get them something."

Frank said, "No! Absolutely not!" He was really adamant. That was like waving a red flag at me and JoAnn, because we saw an opportunity to agitate. Frequently she and I would do that.

We were driving along to Patoka Lake. It seemed like whenever you're on a diet and there's something you're not supposed to have, it's there at every corner. It seemed like we ran across ten doughnut stores. We probably saw only a couple. But, in our minds, every time we turned around, there was another doughnut place. JoAnn would make a crack like, "Oh, boy, I'd love to have that jelly-filled."

And I would say, "Boy, what I wouldn't give for a chocolate-covered, cream-filled doughnut." Frank was getting so angry with us. We were being bad. He started hollering at us, and Lawrence was trying to cool him out.

So we keep driving. We've been going about forty-five minutes. JoAnn and I know we've pushed the button too far, so we stopped. We cool it. We realize we have needled Frank enough. We did have the ability between the two of us to know when to stop, and we did. We stopped teasing him.

But it set the day for Frank. We end up finally getting to Patoka Lake. It seemed like we drove forever. It was a couple of hours. Frank was so aggravated with us he wouldn't even stop to let us use a restroom. We were being punished for being bad.

When we get to the place, we see this beautiful boat dock. It's brand, spanking new. It's going to be a beautiful day. The sun has come up, and it's just gorgeous. There's hardly anybody out there. It was truly a virgin lake. And standing at this dock, was this big, beautiful, brand-new Coca-Cola machine. JoAnn said, "Oh my God, I've got to have a soft drink."

I said, "Me, too, JoAnn. I'm about ready to die!"

We didn't even wait for Lawrence to open the door like he traditionally did. We threw the door open. Both of us went running for the Coca-Cola machine. JoAnn is fumbling in her purse for change. I'm fumbling in mine for change. We get the change out. She puts the money in the machine and pushes the button. We hear clang-clang-clang, and the money came pouring straight out of the machine. I look around behind the machine. It hadn't even been plugged in yet.

That was an omen. That was an omen of things to come.

We started laughing. "Well, that's great." I guess we're really being punished. We knew we'd been a little bad. Not a whole lot; just a little.

We forfeit the idea of having a soft drink. The guys are now backing the boat into the lake. Lawrence and Frank, as much as they liked to fish, were not skilled fishermen. Whenever they did anything like back a boat into water or pull a boat out of water, it always made your heart stop. You'd think, "Are they going to make it, or not?" Because they really, truly were amateurs.

Frank is telling Lawrence, "Do it this way. ... Go here. ... Go there."

Lawrence is going, "Nope. Dad, I'm going to do it this way." They're having debates about how to back the boat into the water. JoAnn and I are standing along the side of the lake. We've got our arms crossed across our chests and we're observing this.

I said, "Boy, doesn't it give you confidence, JoAnn, to know we're going with these experienced fishermen into this unknown lake?"

JoAnn said, "Oh, boy, it really makes me feel good."

Frank ends up walking in the water to unhook this boat, and Lawrence backs the boat into the water. Then Frank gets into the boat. Lawrence parks the car, gets out, and walks into the water to get into the boat. They were trying to angle it out into the lake.

I looked at JoAnn. I said, "JoAnn, I am not going to walk in that water." She said, "Me, neither!"

Frank says, "Come on, girls. Get in the boat."

"Not me. I'm not getting in that way!" I said. "I'm going over on the dock. You all bring the boat to me." I really didn't see any reason why I should get my feet wet. That did not make sense to me. And JoAnn agreed.

Frank is still Mr. Grouchy. He said, "Get in the boat! Both of you, get in the boat. Now!" He's aggravated with us.

JoAnn starts to go. I said, "Don't you dare, JoAnn!" I said, "We're going to get in at the dock."

Lawrence, the peacemaker, is saying, "But, Dad, the girls are right. Why should they get their legs wet?" He said, "They shouldn't get their feet wet. All we have to do is pull the boat over."

"Well, that's ridiculous! It's going to take extra time."

But JoAnn and I held our ground. We refused to get into the water that way. We went and got on the dock. The men brought the boat up to the dock, and we got in that way.

Frank is not real happy with JoAnn and me at all. He's giving us what I would call "sorry looks."

We're on the water. We get in the middle of this bass boat. It had a seat in the front and a seat in the back. Then there was a well you put your fish in. It had a top to it, and you sat down on it just like a seat. That's where JoAnn and I sat.

We go on out into the lake. We're being told all these things about the new rules of this lake. One thing is that there was a game warden who was very careful about checking that everybody had their fishing licenses, and that everybody had everything in the boat you were supposed to have safetywise. There was a very serious fine if you did not have the equipment you needed. Another rule of this lake was your fish had to be twelve inches long, if you caught a bass. If you were caught taking a fish out of this lake less than twelve inches, then you could be fined a big fine and get in some serious trouble. I don't know if it was life imprisonment or what, but I know it was supposed to be pretty serious.

In all the equipment Lawrence Detroy and Frank Haddad had, the one thing they did not have was a ruler. JoAnn says, "How are we going to know if it's twelve inches long?"

I said, "Yeah, Frank, how are we going to know?"

Frank is still grouchy. He's not real happy with us anyway, and he doesn't like us asking questions. He said, "Don't worry about it. We'll figure it out."

Lawrence says, "Dad, my shoe is exactly twelve inches long."

Frank said, "Ah, that's perfect, Fox!"

I said, "Well, wait, wait, wait. ... We're going to catch a fish, and we're going to measure the fish with Lawrence's shoe?"

They both said, like this was normal, "Sure!"

JoAnn and I looked at each other like, "Oh, brother." These are two professional fishermen. We're laughing a little bit. Not out loud! Just subtly, quietly smiling. Snickering inside.

We go on, and we start fishing. Immediately Frank catches a fish. It was a bass. He brings it in. When Frank Haddad fished, and when he would be bringing in a fish, it was hilarious. He had seen every movie on how fishermen bring fish in. He would rip that rod up in the air and flip the arms of the reel, and wind it in. He had all the gyrations perfect. It was like he was bringing in a shark. It was beautiful. He brought that fish in, and it looked big enough. But I questioned the fact that it was twelve inches long.

Lawrence takes his shoe off. Frank lays this pretty, white bass down on the counter there, the well that we were sitting on. He puts Lawrence's shoe beside this fish. Lawrence's shoe was about a fourth of an inch longer than the fish. So Frank takes Lawrence's shoe and pushes it back, to make the tip of the fish's tail even with the tip of Lawrence's shoe.

He says, "It's a keeper."

I said, "Hey! Hey! You cheated! That's not a keeper. You moved the shoe!"

"No I didn't. You don't know what you're talking about."

"I saw you, Frank. You cheated." I said, "That's a cheat. We'll go to jail for this!"

He said, "No we won't! It's a keeper!" And he opened up the lid of the well, and he dropped the fish in the well. "Don't question me! It's a keeper."

JoAnn gives me the eyeball, like, "Don't fight with him!" So we sit back down, and we proceed to start fishing again.

I'm thinking to myself, "He cheated." But we kept on fishing.

JoAnn catches the next fish. Her fish is the twin brother of the fish Frank caught. She brings it in. JoAnn is not as stylish a fisherman as Frank is. She and I both fumbled and bumbled when we would bring in fish. I'm cheering her on. "Come on, JoAnn. You can get it in."

Everybody's yelling at her, "Hold the pole up!" "Hold the pole down!" "Do this!" "Do that!" She brings in this fish. I swear this was exactly the same fish as what was in the well already. This was the twin brother.

Lawrence takes off his shoe. Frank takes the fish off the line, and we lay it down. It also is a fourth of an inch too short. Only this time, it wasn't Mr. Haddad's fish. It was *Mrs.* Haddad's fish. So Mrs. Haddad's fish was illegal. This is what Frank said, "It's not a keeper."

I said, "Is so!" And I pushed Lawrence's shoe back to make it even with the tail of the fish, just like Frank did with his fish.

He said, "You can't do that!"

I said, "Well, you did. And so we're going to."

"Beverly, that is not a keeper."

"If your fish is a keeper, JoAnn's fish is a keeper."

Then JoAnn says, "Yeah, Frank! If you can keep yours, I can keep mine!" We got into this little argument.

Meanwhile, Lawrence is doing everything he can to keep us cool. He's going, "Fellas, it's just a fish! Don't worry about it." He's trying to cool us all out. We're not really mad. We're bantering. We're challenging each other.

Finally, Lawrence opened the well. He said, "Put the fish in the well. It's okay. We'll keep it."

"Well," JoAnn said, "If it's not a keeper, I'm not going to keep it. *And, Mr. Bigshot,* I'm not going to be part of breaking a law. I won't keep a fish that's a fourth of an inch too short! I want the fish put back." She's hollering at Frank about this fish.

Frank takes the fish. But instead of putting it into the well, he flips it out into the lake. He said, "Okay, Mama, that's what we'll do!" So he puts the fish in the lake. And JoAnn doesn't realize that the well is open, and she sits back. She's mad. She's just gonna plop down and pout. So she plops down. The only thing is, the well was open, and she fell into the well filled with water and the twin brother of her fish that's free. Her whole butt is into this well, her feet are up in the air, and her hands are up in the air.

I started laughing, and Frank started hollering. Lawrence is worried

JoAnn's going to drown. But I didn't think she could drown, because her head wasn't in the water.

It was a comical scene to see. She's going, "Get me up! Get me up!" Then she started laughing.

Then Frank ended up giggling. It was funny to see this woman with her feet straight up in the air, and her butt. The water was all the way to her waist. Finally, I'm able to get my composure, and we pulled JoAnn out. By this time she was giggling and laughing, too. Frank slams down the lid of the well. He says, "Both of you! Give me your fishing rods!" He took our fishing rods. We were really bad. When he confiscated our fishing rods, we knew we were in some serious trouble. We hung our heads in shame, because we knew we'd been called on.

He said, "Sit!" So we both sat down. I'll never forget what happened when she sat down. She went *squish*, like that. She was *so* wet. I thought, "Oh God! I've got to sit next to this puddle of water!"

We sit down, and Frank said, "I don't want to hear one more word from either one of you two!" We've got our heads hung because we know we've pushed the button too far. We know we are in serious trouble. Lawrence doesn't even try to intercede. Frank proceeds to tell us that we are not fishermen. He's taking our fishing poles. For the rest of the day, we were not to utter a single sound. Nothing. *Nada.* Just keep our mouths shut.

Well, God had spoken. We both sat there hanging our heads and trying to be real serious. But we can't help the devilish feelings we have in our heart. Even though we know we have sinned and we are being punished by God himself, we think it's funny. In our hearts. We can't stop. We're giggling to each other. But JoAnn's got her head down, and she's going, "Shut up! Shut up, Beverly! Don't say anything! We've pushed him too far!"

I said, "Okay, okay, JoAnn, I'll cool it." So we're both trying hard to obey the new rules that have been given us, and that's to sit and be quiet. Do not interfere with these two sportsmen's fishing.

Then Lawrence and Frank start fishing again. We were in this beautiful little cove. It was a beautiful day. Frank takes his line with an artificial bait. He would zoom that line out and, when he released it, there would be a beautiful hissing sound of the line going far out. He zooms his line out across the lake. There was the cove, and there were trees hanging over the water. Big bass swam notoriously through the spots underneath these trees and branches.

He zips his line across the lake. But instead of going into the water, the line hung up on the branch of a tree. JoAnn and I are sitting there. We see this.

She whispers to me, "Shut up."

I don't say anything. I'm laughing. I'm not laughing out loud. I'm shaking with laughing. I'm giggling inside. I said, "The line's not in the water, JoAnn."

She said, "Shut up! Don't say anything."

Frank was smooth. He was going to pretend. He's not sure whether or not we all know his bait is in the branches of this tree. He's not sure if we paid attention to that. We didn't acknowledge it. We all froze. Lawrence, JoAnn, and I all froze and pretended to not know what was going on. Frank thinks if he could whip his line back a little bit, he could loosen it from the branches of the tree, so it would drop in the water and nobody would know the difference.

He's proceeding with this little gyration. He's pretending to reel in his line, but really he's trying to flip it off the branches of the tree. JoAnn and I are sitting there. She's saying, "Shut up! Shut up! Bev, don't say a thing. Be quiet! Be quiet!"

I'm not saying anything, but I think it's funny.

Two fishermen were in a boat across the lake. One man yells, "Hey, Mister! Do you know your line's in the tree?" Like that. And I mean, that was it.

Frank was furious. He took his knife out. He cut the line, and it went *shoop*. He said, "We're going home. That's it. I've had it! No more fishing today!" He was totally furious because when those guys said that, JoAnn and I burst out laughing. That was not a very nice thing for us to do. I realize that, even to today. That was not a very nice thing to do, to laugh out loud. But we were only human, and it *was* funny.

We decide to proceed to a different area of the lake. Lawrence and

Frank are going on, they're taking the boat, and we're going to some new secret spot that's supposedly a good place to catch fish.

Up to this time, the sky had been beautiful. It was a pretty day. It was just a beautiful day. But all of a sudden, these big, black clouds appear on the horizon. I see it, and JoAnn sees it. We look at each other. We're thinking, "Oh, my God! What is that?"

Up to that time it had been real quiet on the lake, with a bare, subtle breeze. Suddenly the wind starts gusting. The sky begins to get darker and darker. It becomes apparent that a serious storm is on its way. Despite all the joking and the kidding around, the one thing JoAnn Haddad and I have in common is that neither one of us wants to die drowning. That's a big thing with us. Neither one of us can swim, and we're not big on drowning. Our hearts are totally filled with fear, because we see a horrible storm is inevitably coming our way.

JoAnn says, "Lawrence, we need to get the boat back to the dock. It's going to start storming."

Lawrence says, "My God, Frank. The girls are right! Look at the sky!" In an instant, the sky was black. These big, black clouds were rolling in, and we're in the middle of this humongous, deep lake. There were very few people out there. We had life jackets on, but it wasn't enough. I want life jackets, a hoist, and land. That's what I want whenever a bad storm comes. And I would prefer being in a feather bed, and not being out on some lake drowned.

Frank agrees. This is bad. We gather up the gear, and we proceed to go back to the dock. As we're traveling across this lake, we're hitting the water real hard with the boat. There's waves, and you BAM BAM BAM, crash the waves. Then the boat dies. We all look at each other. Frank says, "Did you put gas in the tank, Lawrence?"

Lawrence said, "I don't think I did, Frank." And they had not; the tank was empty. We're in the middle of the lake. The wind is starting to gust. It's getting darker and darker. We know we're going to drown.

Frank said, "Well, we've got some paddles, don't we?" So we look in the boat. There's only one paddle. Frank or Lawrence had it.

JoAnn says, "Well, I'll paddle with my hands!" And so we started to try to paddle with our hands in the water. Frank got the paddle on the other side. We might have had two paddles. Lawrence and Frank maybe each had a paddle. We're trying to paddle with our hands. They're pushing the water.

I'll always remember, Lawrence would say to JoAnn, "JoAnn, cup your hands!" Frank would laugh about this years later. JoAnn put her hand into the water. Her fingers were spread. She was pulling through the water, which was not doing anything. And he's yelling at her to cup her hands so we could get some traction to get the boat moving.

We're not going very far, needless to say. The wind's blowing against us. The waves are starting to get bigger. The storm's coming. We're not moving very far — inches, really. Then, in the distance, we hear a motor running. Across the lake comes this little boat with three people in it: a man, a woman, and a little boy. These people looked like they came from the movie *Deliverance*. The man had greasy hair. He had black grease on his face where he'd been working on a motor or something. His hands were totally black, and his knuckles and fingers were all just — just *black*. His greasy hair was standing straight up. He had one tooth missing in front. The woman looked just about a perfect match to him and the kid. All three of them looked like they had arrived from *Deliverance*.

When they rode up, they were a little bit frightful. They were scary looking. JoAnn was forever suspicious. She said, "Don't accept anything from those people. Don't accept anything. They're probably going to kill us!" We're suspicious.

The strange man says, "You all got problems?"

Well, obviously, we've got problems. We're in the middle of this lake and we can't move. Lawrence had a unique knack of handling most situations. He said, "Yeah, partner." He said, "We've run out of gas. I foolishly didn't check the gas tank, and we ran out of gas. As you see, a storm's coming up. I wonder if you would pull us into the dock."

And the guy just looks at us, like, "Oh, you all are so stupid." Which we were. And then he doesn't comment.

So Lawrence says, "Listen, buddy, I'll fill your gas tank if you'll pull us into the dock."

So the guy looks at his wife, and the two of them look at the kid. Then they nodded at each other like, "Okay, we've got ourselves a good deal here." They throw us a line of rope that they had, and we hold onto the rope. One of the men did, and they proceeded to pull us into the dock.

At the dock, we filled those people's gas tank. They were not bad people at all; they were nice people. We got our boat out of the water, the storm started up, we managed to get our boat hooked up to the car, and we got in the automobile and proceeded to come back to Louisville.

JoAnn and I are still real shook over this situation, because we were pretty close to what we thought was death. It calmed us down and made us cool as far as needling Frank.

It's a good little drive back to Louisville in the car, pulling the boat behind us. We get all the way to Spaghetti Junction in Louisville, and Frank's spirits are better. I think we did stop and get something to eat real quick. That was like the biggest thing you could do for Frank Haddad to settle down his grouchy mood. Everybody was kind of giddy and kind of happy, because when you feel like you've almost been hurt but you got out of it, you feel better. You feel good. We were laughing and telling stories between the four of us, jiving and stuff. We're on Spaghetti Junction and we're going around that turn where you come off the Indiana bridge over to Louisville. That big Spaghetti Junction turn there.

We're on the expressway, coming off of the bridge. Frank is looking back at JoAnn. He was telling us something. All of a sudden, the color drained from his face. His large brown eyeballs got bigger, and he was staring over my shoulder. I was on the left side in the back and JoAnn was on the right. He's staring over my shoulder out the window. He's got this horrified look in his eyes. He started saying, "Fox! Fox! Oh, Fox!"

Lawrence said, "Yeah, Dad, what's up?"

Lawrence was driving along. He's just cool as a cucumber. I go and look over my shoulder. The darn boat had snapped off the chain and it was hanging on. When he hooked the boat up to the car, we had a boat hitch, and we used a chain to the boat hitch. Then he used a safety rope besides that. The boat was hanging by the safety rope only. The boat hitch had broken. The boat was loose! Looking out our windows, the boat was going at an angle from our automobile.

Lawrence looks in the rear-view mirror and he sees it, too.

JoAnn looks over and, she sees it. She's screaming bloody murder. We know we're in trouble. You're going on the expressway, you're on a turn, naturally your car is picking up speed, so we've got a loose boat on the back of the automobile.

Anyway, I'll always know at least something about Lawrence Detroy. When the heat hit, that's when he was strongest. He could always handle bad situations, and when things were really horrible, someway or another, he was his coolest.

Lawrence said, "Don't worry about it, y'all. We'll be okay."

Well, Frank is saying, "Lawrence, get the car off the road! Get the car off the road!" But you couldn't get the car off the road, with that trailer and boat. There were vehicles behind us, vehicles in front of us. There was too much speed, and the boat started swaying from side to side. It went to one side of the road and back over to the other. It's forcing us to pick up more speed.

There was a man in a little pickup truck behind us, and he saw everything. The people in front of us don't know what's going on. Anyway, this man started driving from one side to the other, of the lanes, and he put on his emergency lights and slowed down real slow to make all the cars slow down behind us. He's laying on his horn, trying to stop everybody behind us. Another car could come right up on you, and the boat would swerve over and knock the other car. It would be a horrific wreck.

JoAnn was screaming bloody murder.

Lawrence is saying, "JoAnn, calm down! I'm trying to think!" He's trying to drive and keep his cool. JoAnn couldn't stop screaming. I put my hand over JoAnn's mouth.

I said, "JoAnn, please, please try. PLEASE calm down! Please don't scream. Lawrence is trying to drive!"

Frank is trying to be co-pilot. He tells Lawrence, "The boat's over here! The boat's over there!" He's trying to guide Lawrence, too.

The car's going very fast. JoAnn finally nodded her head that she was going to stop screaming. I'll always remember. I took my hand, and I lifted it off her face. She goes, "Ahhhh!" Then she started screaming again. I put my hand back on her face.

I said, "PLEASE, JoAnn, please! You're distracting Lawrence. We need the pilot to be able to pilot this aircraft."

We drove almost to the Zorn Avenue exit before we could slow the car down. Lawrence finally was able to ease over into the emergency lane. Then he just went very, very, very slow. It seemed like it was forever before he was finally able to stop the vehicle. The entire time, the only thing that kept this boat from breaking loose was a little nylon safety rope Frank and Lawrence had bantered about whether they'd even use it on the back of the car.

Finally we came to a stop. We're in the emergency lane, and the guys get out. JoAnn and I are sitting in the back seat. We are absolutely, practically on the floor. It was horrible what happened. I thought to myself, "God is punishing us! We have been such bad sinners that we deserved this punishment."

They finally re-anchored the boat to the car. We got home safely. But I'll tell you what. Fishing is a dangerous game, I don't care what anybody says.

"Bev, I'm Going Under!"

Lawrence and I were newly married. Friends of ours, Joe Gales and Tony Gargotta, loved to fish at Herrington Lake. Gargotta had a cabin down there. Lawrence loved fishing down there. We had a bass boat, and we had agreed to go fishing for a couple of days at Herrington Lake.

It was in the fall. It was very cold, and it had rained the night before. Fishermen always have little gimmicks and tricks they use. Gargotta swore that when it rained, the fish would be biting better the following morning. Probably he was right, because we did have good luck when we fished after a rain.

There weren't many people down at Herrington Lake. Herrington Lake is absolutely gorgeous. But it's very treacherous. It's extremely deep. It's a very dangerous lake.

We arrived early in the morning just as the sun was coming up. Nobody was out on the lake but Tony and Joe. Joe Gales was quite a character. Tony was like a rough fisherman. He was a khakis-and-more-casual fisherman. But Gales was slick. He had a bass boat flecked in red and silver, metallic silver. He had fishing gear that was red and silver. This guy was so coordinated it was pitiful.

I remember seeing them already out on the lake and thinking, "My God, what time did they get up to get here?" The sun was just coming up. It was still fairly dark.

We get out on the lake, and they're motioning to us. We're pretty far away at the dock. They're waving for us to hurry up. They had found a spot guaranteed to be *the* spot, the basic spot where fishermen know the fish are. We wanted to get to this spot, and they wanted to get there, before any other fishermen got out. They were known to be good fishermen, and they didn't want to tip off the secret place.

They're motioning for us to hurry up. There was a houseboat on the lake, and the houseboat had gone across from one side to the other, leaving rough waves in its wake. It was a series of real heavy waves and currents. The downpour the night before had brought up a lot of debris from this very, very deep lake. And Lawrence was going too fast across the lake to catch up with the guys we could see off in the distance.

All of a sudden we felt this *thump*. Our boat flipped over. Both of us flipped out into the water, about twenty feet apart. I hit the water so hard I broke my hand. I had on a life jacket, but could not swim. I cannot swim at all. Lawrence didn't have his life jacket, and he couldn't swim either.

The boat landed on its belly after flipping. It started circling Lawrence and me. We were about twenty feet apart. I'm terrorized. I know I'm going to drown. The water is green and mucky and freezing cold. I thought I'd die. Then it occurred to me Lawrence can't swim. And he's worried about me, but we're too far away to help one another. The boat is circling us because the motor is still going. Every time it circled us, it would swoop a little bit closer. We kept trying to tread closer to one another to keep from being chopped up by the motor.

Gales and Gargotta see this happen, and they ease up to us. But they can't get too close. They don't want to throw the boat off the track it's on, where it could get one or the other of us. So Lawrence is not able to swim. And he has only a partial lung because of the TB he had as a youth. He goes under the water. I'm thinking he's drowning. He comes back up and treads water. He kept telling me, "Calm down! Calm down! You're going to be okay!" Then he'd say, "Alright, I'm going under! I'm going under, but don't worry — I'll be back." Then he'd go under the water.

Meanwhile the boat would be swooping past us. There's no control of the boat. There's nobody in the boat. I'm thinking, "He's drowned, he's drowned! Oh my God, he's drowned!" Then I thought, "Oh hell, I'm going to drown, too!"

Then he'd come bobbing back up again. He'd bob back up again and tread water for a little while. Then he'd say, "Alright — I'm going under. And I'll be back."

This went on for five minutes or so. It seemed like an eternity. Finally the motor died down, and Tony and Joe were able to get to us. They hauled us into their boat. We got back to the dock.

When we got back to the dock, people had already called for help. They said the only thing that saved us was the fact we didn't know how to swim. They said a lot of people had drowned in Herrington Lake because they thought they were good swimmers and thought they could get to shore. All we did was tread water and pray.

V. GANG AT PLAY

Christmas Party
The Shower Scene
No Popcorn for JoAnn
"The Godfather"
Culture
Frank Haddad, the Chef
Chili-Off
Derby

CHRISTMAS PARTY

The four of us went to James Scott's Christmas party. It's JoAnn and me, and Frank and Lawrence.

Twelve years earlier, Scott had been convicted of manslaughter in the death of his wife, and had served a year and a half in prison before the governor commuted his 21-year sentence. More recently, Frank had persuaded a special judge to overturn Scott's conviction, because the medical testimony of two doctors about repeated blows to her head with a blunt instrument had been recanted or reinterpreted, and the current state medical examiner categorically concluded, "Mr. Scott could not have committed the crime in the fashion under which he was convicted." At all times, Scott had contended his wife had been drinking and fell in the bathroom, striking her head on the bathtub.

So the four of us were at James Scott's home. Everybody else is a little clique. We don't fit in with the guests. They're all bluebloods, and they're married to bluebloods. They would say things like, "Well, I was married to him, but then I married his cousin, and then the niece did that." It was so confusing keeping up with all these people. And they had names like Angus, for cattle or whatever.

But we're dealing with it. And they're looking at us like we're fascinating, because we're normal people out on the street. They're asking us everything. Lawrence had all kinds of stories. Frank had all kinds of stories. Lawrence was a bondsman, and Frank was Louisville's acclaimed criminal defense attorney.

So they're fascinated with us. We felt like we were specimens. The house was beautiful. It was an absolutely gorgeous mansion. It had room after room of antique furniture, and settees, and mirrors. A gorgeous place.

There was a little buffet in the dining room. We went through the buffet, one by one. There were twenty or thirty people. They all sat down on the floor to eat. I'm holding my plate.

JoAnn said, "Everybody's sitting on the floor."

I said, "Not me."

"But everybody else is."

"I don't care, JoAnn. There are chairs. I'm going to use a chair. It's the way I was brought up. I'm not sitting on the floor."

Frank says, "If I sat down on the floor, you'd have to get a hoist to get me back up again!"

The four of us sat on a settee. We held our plates in our laps. Everybody stopped talking. The room got silent. We had committed the biggest faux-pas. They just started looking at us. JoAnn said, "I guess we're in trouble now."

I said, "I don't care. I'm eating."

One by one they all got up and found chairs. I thought, maybe they didn't know about chairs. Maybe they didn't know what furniture was for.

I always thought Jim Scott was innocent. I believed Frank, and he told me Jim was innocent. Almost everything Frank told me I believed.

But after the trial, and after he had served time, and after the governor had released him, and Frank had worked the case so well, Jim wanted to design a staircase for Lawrence in the Evening News. The Evening News later became the Downtowner. It was a club downtown. Lawrence wanted the staircase to look like it had always been there, because the fire marshal wouldn't let us put one in.

The staircase had to look like it had been there forever, and the fire marshal just missed it. Jim Scott's job as an architect was to design this incognito staircase. The building was from the 1800s, so he had to blend it in.

He called one night and said, "Got the design done."

I thought, "The design for what?"

He said, "For the staircase. I'd like you and Lawrence to come over."

I said, "Okay, we'll come over."

So we go over. The Indian Hills neighborhood is rich and elegant. It's raining. It's late Fall. It's cold. It's pitch black. It's spooky. It's out of those old black and white movies. We go in. I'd never been upstairs. All the times I'd been in his house, I'd only been downstairs. Jim said, "Well, we'll go upstairs to the sitting room."

I thought, "Ding! Ding! Ding! Sitting room? Oh no, I don't want to go there." That's me. But, I kept my cool. I said, "Alright, whatever you want."

We went upstairs to this little sitting room. It was a beautiful room with a fireplace. It had antique needlepoint work. Everything was gorgeous. Trees brushed up against a little window over to the side. I told Lawrence, "If ever there was a setting for a murder, this is it now!" Jim went downstairs to get chili. He served this chili in a silver tureen. Have you ever had chili in a silver tureen? That's pretty much the formal way to do it.

I'm getting nervous. I'm not really feeling comfortable. I think, this is it. Nobody will even know Lawrence and I were here. Who would look for us in the blueblood's house? So I said, "Jim, I've got to go to the restroom." I know where the restroom is downstairs.

But he said, "Well, use my bathroom."

I said, "No! I don't want to use your bathroom. I want to go downstairs to the bathroom I know." I know that his bathroom is *the* bathroom — the scene of the death.

He says, "Ah, no, Beverly." I turned white as a ghost. Lawrence is kicking me. He's thinking I'm being obvious.

Jim said, "No, no. Use my bathroom. It's right at the end of the hallway."

I thought, "Oh, no." But I'm trying to be polite. I go down this hallway. The house is dark, you know. These people have beautiful furniture. But they don't believe in electricity. It's pitch-black. It's beautiful though, but spooky-beautiful.

I go down the hallway. I see this little light in a doorway. It's the last room on the right. I see a small light. I thought he said it's the last room, so I go down there. There are two big, enormous beds with canopies. Gorgeous, gorgeous beds. And in the middle of these two beds is an oil painting of Eloise, with a light on it. I'm going, "Oh my God, he's got a monument to her!" The light is left on like a perpetual light for Eloise. I'm thinking, "Oh well, I'm being picky." I was getting a little nervous.

I go into the bathroom. On the counter was an unbelievable amount of beautiful, silver antique-framed pictures of Eloise with the baby, Eloise at the party, Eloise at the track, Eloise, Eloise, Eloise. There were no pictures of the kids, nothing. It was a monument. He didn't have toothpaste on the counter. The walls were covered with framed pictures of Eloise too.

When I came out, I told Lawrence, "Look at the blueprints. Approve them. Let's leave."

Later I told Frank. I said, "Frank, he did it."

He said, "Oh Beverly, you're wrong."

I said, "The next time you go over to Jim's house, I want you to use his bathroom upstairs."

"Oh, you're exaggerating."

"I'm not exaggerating, Frank!"

The next time we go, he says, "Jim, I'm going to use your restroom. I'll go upstairs."

He goes upstairs, and I'm telling you, Haddad came running down the stairs. He was hotfootin' it. He said, "He did do it!"

That was the spooky thing.

THE SHOWER SCENE

The four of us, Frank and JoAnn and Lawrence and me, dearly loved to go to the movies together. Frank and I had the same fondness for popcorn, and Frank was a gourmet popcorn-popper. We generally enjoyed a movie with bullets and lots of shooting. Any time the name Charles Bronson or Clint Eastwood came up, or John Wayne, further back, the guys wanted see their movies. Frank would pop popcorn at home and put it in brown paper bags, with seasoning and butter, and shake the bags up, so we went to the theater with our own stash of popcorn.

At the movies, the four of us always laughed. We always got in trouble. It never failed. People around us seemed to join in with us. But one time was a particularly funny time. We laughed for years. This was when the movie *Dressed to Kill* came out with Michael Caine.

He played a psychiatrist-sociopath who dressed up as a woman to kill people. Angie Dickinson was the star of this movie, and she had a shower scene. The shower scene was publicized a lot. Lawrence and Frank both had enormous crushes on this woman. She was beautiful. She played the Policewoman on TV. Both these guys loved her. They couldn't wait to get to this movie to see this shower scene that was publicized so well.

We get in the theater. The place was packed. We find seats fairly close to the front. And we had our popcorn. We're all settled in, ready to go. JoAnn and I are laying the needle about this shower scene's coming up. Lawrence says, "I'll go get us some Cokes. I'll be right back."

Well he goes for the Cokes. But the place was so packed he had to wait in line to get the soft drinks. By the time he got them, the movie had already started. We're sitting up close to the front. Down comes Lawrence. Frank is giggling, because Lawrence is missing part of the movie. We're laying the needle about the Fox being so slow. It wasn't his fault. He was tied up in the line.

So he gets down to our seats. He turns his back to the screen. He starts trying to get his gear together to hand to us. He was the soul of kindness to get us these soft drinks. Behind him, on the screen, was the shower scene he wanted to see, Angie Dickinson in the shower. The movie shows all of this beautiful woman. First the silhouette of her body through the shower door, and then she's washing herself and everything. The whole time Lawrence has got his back to the screen. He's going, "Here, Frank!" and he's handing Frank a Coke. He passes it down, and then, "Here, JoAnn!"

He was so careful, so kind and considerate. He handed us each our soft drinks, each our straws, each a napkin. Meanwhile, the shower scene's going on. He's missing the entire thing. Frank is sitting in his seat dying laughing, because his friend is missing the very scene he came to see. By the time Lawrence sat down, the movie had moved on to generalized murder.

Through the whole movie, Frank was giggling and laughing that the Fox missed this one scene. As we're leaving, Lawrence said, "Frank, I didn't think that scene was that good with Angie." He never did see *the scene*. He saw another scene where a towel was being handed to somebody.

We laughed for years about poor Lawrence standing there so patiently, and meanwhile Angie's in the shower doing her thing, and he missed the whole thing. It went over his head.

No Popcorn for JoAnn

I love my friend JoAnn. But JoAnn's reputation for picking movies is not really so good.

When the movie *The Alien* came out, Frank said, "You know JoAnn. She listens to everybody when they say it's a good movie."

She was sold on *The Alien* and told us, "We've gotta go see this movie! Everybody says it's great. We've gotta go!" She's real insistent. We don't know anything about the movie because it's brand, spanking new. We're standing in line.

I'm looking around, and we're surrounded by kids. I said, "JoAnn, what's this movie about?"

She said, "You know, it's an alien. You know, about people from another country."

Then Frank says, "JoAnn, are you sure this movie's for adults? What is this movie?" Young kids crowded all around.

She said, "No, no. It's really supposed to be exciting."

We get inside the theater with our usual stash of popcorn. We're sitting down. The first scene is ridiculous. It shows something that looks like a shrimp and this alien stuff. They pop out of these pods, like eggs emerging. It's the birth scene of the alien. JoAnn's sitting between Frank and me. She realizes she's picked a movie that's not quite what we thought it was going to be. She starts sinking in her chair. Frank and I looked over to her from both sides and gave her a very cold look.

Then we watched the movie again. Some other horrible scene happened with some alien thing coming out of somebody's stomach. We proceeded to berate poor JoAnn about her selection of the movie. Frank finally got absolutely aggravated by the movie he considered to be completely stupid. We weren't science fiction people.

Suddenly, Frank grabs JoAnn's popcorn. He said, "That's it! Your popcorn's confiscated." He seizes her popcorn. I'm helping Frank.

We're both needling poor JoAnn. I said, "Well, JoAnn, I hope you can find a way home. I'm sure there'll be somebody around who'll be able to take you home." We wanted to kill her. The movie was so lousy.

Poor Lawrence was sitting there. He says, "I don't understand it, Dad! What the hell's this movie about, anyway?" He couldn't understand. He wanted to see Clint Eastwood or Charles Bronson. He didn't want to see some kind of weird-looking shrimps or worms killing people.

Some guy is sitting behind us in the theater. He feels sorry for JoAnn. He thinks she's being brutalized. When this movie finally ended, and we were leaving in total disgust, JoAnn was hanging her head because she was a bad girl. She had picked a horrible movie. This guy tapped her on the shoulder and said, "Mrs. Haddad, I'll give you a ride home."

"The Godfather"

When *The Godfather*, the first movie, came out, Lawrence and I and Jeanette and Bob Woolsey and Frank and JoAnn went to see it. *The Godfather* was such a good movie. This time, instead of having popcorn, we took a picnic lunch. We had grapes and kubbi and cheese, and a basket full of treats. The kubbi was fresh-baked. You could smell it. It was just wonderful, with pine nuts in the center. We might even have had some wine. Jeanette might have brought some wine.

We made it an event. Whenever we went to the movies, it was an event. We went into the theater. We settle in. We open up our packages. When we opened up that kubbi, people started falling out of the seats around us. It smelled so good. Everybody was hanging on. They pleaded, "Oh, please, let me have some!" It was a terrific event.

When we got back after the kubbi picnic, poor Queenie the dog had been hit in front of the Haddad house. We drove up, after we thoroughly had a ball at the movie, and had pretty much broken all the rules of the theater about not bringing in food, which was our style. But when we drove up to the Haddad house, a crowd had gathered out in the street. In their midst lay a big pile of fur that was obviously Queenie. Queenie had been hit by a car.

I'll always remember. Frank's son Frankie picked up that collar. He was just so very sad that Queenie had been killed. But Queenie had gotten old. She would wander out in the road. She chased cars, too. Whenever I see *The Godfather* movie, I always think of Queenie the collie. It's a hard thing to put together. But that's the way it is.

CULTURE

One time we decided we were going to get some culture. We got the guys to take us to see a play. It was at the Brown. That wasn't Lawrence's cup of tea. Frank tolerated it. But JoAnn and I wanted to go see this play.

We went to see this play. It was pretty depressing, a horrible play, about an alcoholic father and a dope-addict mother, and dysfunction. The whole family was dysfunctional. Actually, the whole play was nonsensical. It was really stupid.

Lawrence tried to be polite. We had the best seats in the Brown. Everybody dressed beautifully. It was like an event. About five minutes into the play, anybody could see where it was going.

Lawrence clears his throat and says, "Excuse me, Dad. I'm going to go to the restroom. Excuse me." So he eases on out the row, goes up the aisle, and leaves. About five minutes later, it becomes apparent Lawrence isn't returning.

Frank says, "Uh, JoAnn, uh, Beverly, uh, I'll be right back," and he disappears.

We're sitting there, JoAnn and I. We're watching the play. It got stupider by the minute. Pretty soon, JoAnn and I walked out of the theater, and that was the end of culture.

Lawrence said, "Why would people pay good money to see all this dysfunctional family stuff?" He said it didn't make sense to him. He didn't need culture that bad, to be subjected to that.

Frank Haddad, the Chef

One of Frank Haddad's favorite things was eating. He loved anything to do with food. Lawrence and Frank and a group of friends held fish fries. Frank would barbecue ribs on occasion, and it was quite an honor to be invited to his house to eat his ribs.

When he cooked, he put his apron on. He had a big, round belly like Santa Claus. He would stand by the grill as he fried the fish or baked the ribs or chicken. He was always on a diet. Frank perpetually was on a diet. But he would manage, as he cooked, to have a taste. Good cooks have to know their food is quality. He would eat a bite and put some on a platter, eat a bite and put some on a platter.

Their dog Queenie was still alive at the time. Everybody loved this collie. Frankie and Debbie adored this Queenie. She would sit beside Frank when he was cooking, especially when he cooked ribs. She looked at him with these loving eyes. Frank would eat a bite, and then he would throw Queenie a bite. So Queenie would sit there all day long. Queenie was a big dog.

When Frank would sit down to eat after cooking at the grill, he would take only a limited portion because he was watching his weight.

He had all kinds of seasonings he liked to fool with. Of course, his father had run a butcher store, and he had worked in the butcher store, so he knew a lot about seasonings and meats.

JoAnn said she never really knew what was in the seasoning. Twice a year, he made a seasoning that I nicknamed "Mystery X." Frank would get together all of his fresh spices and seasonings. He would go down in the basement and close the door. He'd wear a white apron. JoAnn called him the mad scientist. Occasionally, she'd open the door and smoke would come billowing up from the fresh seasonings. She'd say, "Frank, are you alright?"

He'd answer, "Yeah, I'm fine, Mama Jo. I'm fine."

Then at the end of the afternoon, he'd come up with all these jars of seasoning he'd made. The seasoning was so awesome. "Mystery X" was good on salads. I used it on everything: fish, poultry and pork. My little nephew was the pickiest eater when he was about three, and I gave him some of Frank's seasoning to put on some eggs, and this kid, from that day on, got his own supply of "Mystery X." It was difficult to get on the list to receive "Mystery X" to start with. But Frank sent him his own supply, and he hid it at his own house. His poor mother would say, "Colin, where's the Mystery X?"

Colin had it hidden somewhere. He'd say, "I'll get it." He'd go get it and then sprinkle it in whatever Leontia was fixing. Then he'd hide it somewhere again. Even his mother didn't have access to this "Mystery X."

I still have some. I don't know how long it'll last. But I'll always treasure the memory of Frank making these seasonings. The other thing he loved to make was peppers. He had wonderful pickled peppers that you could put with anything.

CHILI-OFF

Frank liked to compete with his cooking. He would try to top JoAnn. They would have their "chili-offs" between JoAnn's chili and Frank's chili.

Frank would do anything he could to sabotage JoAnn's chili. He'd secretly add ingredients to her chili when she was occupied with guests. But Lawrence, ever loyal to his friend JoAnn no matter what, would always say JoAnn's chili was the best. Whenever a lot of people were voting on whose chili was the best, Lawrence always leaned toward his buddy. He knew Frank would get a lot of votes just because of who he was.

One time, Frank was really working hard to make his pot of chili better than JoAnn's. Lawrence came up and said, "Dad, you know yours isn't bad, but JoAnn's is really good."

Frank got so aggravated with Lawrence. He could have killed him. JoAnn won that chili-off. But Frank was a great cook.

DERBY

Every year, for twenty-five years, we went to the track with Frank and JoAnn Haddad and Judy and Morris Brown. We were three couples who thoroughly enjoyed each other's company. Morris and Lawrence and Frank were so funny together. And Judy and JoAnn and I just had a ball.

We loved watching the people. We'd sit in our box and look at everybody's outfits. Sometimes we'd spot a celebrity or see some local politician. We saw a lot of regulars and people we knew, year in and year out. People would come by the box and talk to us. Every year, we looked forward to the arrival of Frank and JoAnn's friends, the Georges. They'd bring a bag of kubbi, which was just absolutely wonderful. His mother would make this kubbi, and we looked forward to getting that. Judy would have glorious sandwiches: country ham and roast beef, and little cocktail buns, and grape leaves. We had a ball. We'd sit there and have this picnic lunch. Frank's life centered on food. He loved it. If there was food, he was satisfied.

So we would open up these packages of picnic lunch, and people would come by. And there were other couples that were friends of ours at the track. Frank always invited Carter and Sue Phillips from Virginia to come down. They loved to come for Derby. The Browns entertained a lot of people associated with his Cadillac dealership and friends from all around. It was a lot of fun.

We would have a mint julep. It was always an annual thing. They would come around with mint juleps, and we'd toast one another. We'd giggle and tell stories.

One man had a little bar. He was a bald-headed, little guy. He couldn't have been more than five feet tall. His wife had died. Every year for several years in a row, he would seek us out. JoAnn and I would sit there thinking, "Oh no, here he comes." He would stand there and buy us a drink and toast his dead wife. Then he'd start crying. Every year it was the same thing. "Oh I miss my wife!" We'd sit there and sympathize with him.

We dearly loved our tradition of riding a limousine out to the track on Derby day. Judy would want to use the Brown Brothers limousine. But just getting in the limousine was a killer. It always challenged us. Although it sounds glamorous, no matter how big the car's supposed to be, it's uncomfortable to fit several couples into it. We would have to angle and wiggle in the seats. We'd place our legs just so, so we wouldn't hit the person's legs across the aisle and cause a runner in someone's hose. And when we would get in the car, there'd be a tremendous amount of giggling and laughing because we're positioning ourselves for the long ride to the track.

Frank was very sharp. He'd ride up front with Morris and the chauffeur, and give the chauffeur directions to the track.

Morris would give one set of directions. Frank would give another. Judy would pipe in with her advice. Lawrence would suggest, "Well, why don't we go this way?" It's a miracle we ever made it to the track. The poor chauffeur had all these individuals giving him advice. I know he was trying to be polite and just get us to the track. This job had to be the worst job of all of the chauffeurs. They probably drew straws, and whoever got the short straw had to take the Browns and the Detroys and the Haddads to the track.

But after we got in the car and got settled and everything, our attention turned to the amenities. There was a bar in the car with crystal decanters. The decanters were *so* heavy. They were like a hundred pounds to me. Inevitably I sat next to the decanters. Lawrence would be on one side, by the ice. He would get the cups out and put ice in the cups. Judy would hold the cup, and Lawrence would put the ice in the cups. Then they'd pass the drinks to me. I would pour either vodka or bourbon into the cup. For me to get that liquor into the glass was a virtual miracle in the moving vehicle, because the car was vibrating the whole time. I got all kinds of advice from everybody. "Not too much." "A little bit more." Then we would get rid of the decanter and move on to tonic or orange juice, or whatever the side drink was to be in the glass. And last, we would top the drink with a lemon or a lime. We'd squish it around the edge and squeeze it in, and then we'd pass these drinks.

This was all very synchronized, so everybody would get a drink. We'd pass a couple up to Frank and Morris. Each of us would get a cocktail. Then we would toast the day's event, the Derby. We'd laugh and tell stories. Most times we made it to the track pretty even, but on occasion, we'd be stuck in traffic. Several times, when the city decided to do construction work, that would throw off all the lines of traffic, so we were narrowed down in the streets we could use. We ended up sitting and sitting and sitting, trying to get to the track in this mass of people. When we sat, we drank. We would end up just absolutely giggling and carrying on. I don't want to say we got drunk, but we got awfully high. Frank was hilarious when he would get mellow.

Judy Brown always dressed so elegant and beautiful. One year, she wore an emerald green suit with an emerald green hat that was beautiful. Judy with her black hair and dark eyes and Indian looks is such a beautiful woman anyway. Frank decides he wants to try on Judy Brown's hat. This was probably after three drinks. Her hat was a big, wide-brimmed hat. Judy passes her hat up to Frank, and Frank puts it on. We were edging closer to the track, and a group of people was standing on the side of the walk, waiting to get into the track. They started yelling about who was in this limousine.

They couldn't see in because the windows were all tinted. But we could see out. When Frank pushed the button down for the window to open, the crowd said, "There's Frank Haddad!" He was wearing Judy's emerald green hat. I don't know what those people thought, but I'm sure there were tremendous rumors for ages. But we all died. We were going, "Oh my God, put the window *up*, Frank, please!" We would just have a really good time, harmless fun, going to the track.

Then when we got there, the guys were so scientific the way they bet.

They had their racing forms. They had their advice from other people who were very knowledgeable about what horse was going to win. Different people would come up to them and say, "Oh, in race such-and-such, so-and-so's going to win." The men are marking it down.

Judy and JoAnn and I were also scientific. We went by the color of the silks, the name of the horse. If the horse had a long tail, that was always a big clue. We went by things like that. The guys bet in the big windows, and the women bet in the two-dollar windows. But we equally had fun. And the truth is, we won just as much as the guys did, with all of their scientific knowledge and advice and knowledgeable people. Our technique was as good as theirs as far as winning. We did win a lot. Not big money, but for us it was a lot. We enjoyed it.

After Derby day at the track, getting out was always a killer. Then we would go to Judy's house for a dinner to continue the fun. Judy would have a lot of guests at her house. Her house was beautiful. Frank loved to get in people's kitchens. He was horrible. We would get to her big, beautiful kitchen, and Frank would open up drawers and analyze what kind of utensils she had. JoAnn and I would be going, "Frank! Get out of Judy's drawers! Leave those! Get out of that stuff. Now, leave it alone!"

And he said, "I just want to see what she uses here." He would absolutely immerse himself in poor Judy's kitchen.

And Judy was just like, "Oh, brother!"

Then his thing was, if she had tenderloin or country ham, or whatever she had, he sliced it. Of course, whenever Frank would slice meat, and portion it out, that meant he had to taste it. The whole time he's slicing it, one piece goes on the platter and one piece went in his stomach. We had many, many beautiful Derbies together, sitting around the table eating this delightful food that the Browns prepared. We enjoyed conversations with the variety of guests who were there. We always tried to get Lawrence and Frank to tell a story. Sometimes we'd heard the story several times over, but every time we would all just die laughing. They were funny men, and they were funniest when they'd tell a story. Frank would start it. Then he'd pass it off to Lawrence. He'd pipe in and tell his part and then pass it back to Frank. They had it like a song and dance routine. But they used to mesmerize us with all their adventures and stories.

VI. LAWRENCE AND BEVERLY IN ITALY

Statue of David
Comic Opera

Statue of David

When Lawrence had his clubs and cocktail lounges, he was a member of the Liquor Dealers' Association. Occasionally, the Liquor Dealers would sponsor junkets to various parts of the country, and abroad, like in Europe.

One year, they sponsored a trip to Rome, and we decided to go. It was a year or two before we were married.

Probably two hundred people were on that trip. The majority were liquor dealers and nightclub operators from Louisville and Chicago and various places in this part of the country. The majority were Jewish, with very few Gentiles. But we knew a lot of the people, and it was a *long* flight to Rome.

We went to Rome, and we stayed in a charming little hotel. A lot of the other people on the trip were horrified because the rooms were little. But I liked the idea of a tiny hotel in the heart of Rome. We could look out the windows and see all the activity on the streets. There were street vendors and flower carts and people selling jewelry on the street. There were sidewalk cafes and a lot of hustling and bustling about. I liked that. I liked to be able to watch the activities from the window of our hotel room.

We had a friend in Rome. Her name was Michelle. She was a friend of Little Larry's. Michelle worked for oil company executives in Rome.

Michelle Renzi is Italian. She comes from an Italian family. She spoke very fluent Italian, and she was thrilled we'd be there from her home city of

Louisville. Her boss gave her the use of a company car, a Mercedes-Benz, to take us around Rome while we were there.

It was really a neat thing to do. In the mornings, the Liquor Dealers' Association had our whole agenda planned out. You go on this tour; you go on that tour. Lawrence was not a tour person, and neither was I. So in the morning, they would have continental breakfasts, and we would skip the breakfast. Michelle would be there to pick us up. Then she would give us her tour of Rome. She lived in Rome. She knew parts of Rome that were not the tourist Rome. She knew the real Rome. She would take us to neat restaurants and places. We had a lot of fun.

Michelle was very pretty and attractive and she'd drive up in this silver Mercedes-Benz and park out front. She'd jump out of the car and greet us. After several days of this, one particular couple in our group just could not understand who was this person that was picking us up every day. The wife was so jealous-hearted and complained about everything. They were so snippy. Lawrence, forever the agitator, loved to stir people up. The woman was very nosy. She'd want to know, if we weren't going to eat our continental breakfast, could she have our rolls? She absolutely got on both Lawrence's and my nerves. After traveling on this long trip, she became irritating to us.

The husband and wife watched Michelle come get us. So finally the guy went up to Lawrence and said, "So who is this woman who picks you all up every day?"

Lawrence measured the guy. "Well, hell," he said, "she's a tour guide."

"A tour guide? In a Mercedes-Benz?"

"Yeah, that's all they had left." He said, "I worked out a deal with the company. I pay her ten bucks a day and she picks Beverly and me up and takes us all over Rome."

This guy absolutely had a fit. Where could he get a tour guide like this Italian beauty for ten dollars a day? His wife was not only mean, but ugly, and he wasn't so much himself. He had to live with his evil and jealous-hearted wife. She probably could have been attractive if she didn't have so much vindictiveness and hatefulness about her. He sees this really beautiful woman. Michelle was built really pretty and wore gorgeous designer clothes and spoke fluent Italian. She laughed and mingled and knew people. And she's a tour guide for ten dollars a day? It absolutely killed this couple who were just so jealous-hearted.

Then Lawrence told Michelle, and Michelle went along. This guy asked her, "Can we hire anybody like you or anything?"

Michelle went on and made a big deal about it. "No, I was the last one," and "There's nobody else available." and "It's too bad you didn't contact me in time." She helped fan the fire with Lawrence. And this couple who were so jealous-hearted spent all their time talking about us. They'd say, how dare we? We did not go on any of the tours that they offered, except for one.

I wanted to see the statue of David. I had studied art at Murray. I love art. I thought the statue of David was beautiful. It was something I felt I had to see. The statue of David was in Florence in a museum. Florence was eighty miles away.

One of the tours this organization planned was a bus trip to Venice for the day and on to Florence to see the statue of David. Lawrence did not want to take the bus trip. He did not like the tours. He didn't like some of the people in this organization (especially the irritating couple). But I wanted to do it, and he relented. He said, "Okay, I'll go on the tour."

We go downstairs early. The bus was out front. People were boarding. The tour guide was a stocky-built man. He looked like a military man. He acted like a military man. Lawrence was never in the military, and he was not a military-thinking man. He was free and easy, and he did things his own way. He never could enjoy being bossed, and he never would permit anyone to bully him.

The tour guide had learned English off of a record. It was obvious. His speech was rigid. He would say things like, "Everybody must be on the bus at 2:05. I said 2:05. Not 2:06, but 2:05. If you are not on the bus, we will leave without you." He barked all these orders to us. I could feel instantly Lawrence did not like this guy. But he had agreed to do what I wanted to do, to go and see the statue of David. So he went along with the deal and we got on the bus. We settled in. We were driving through a beautiful part of the country around Rome. There were olive gardens. It was lovely. We saw vineyards and open meadows. The tour guide talked into a microphone. He looked back at all of us on the bus. There were probably thirty or forty people. There was not an empty seat on the bus. He pointed out different landmarks to look at.

I knew we were in trouble because we were looking out the window to the left. We were looking at an olive orchard filled with all these big, beautiful olive trees. I was telling Lawrence how beautiful it was. "Isn't that lovely?"

The tour guide is pointing out something on the right. He said, "And on your right is...." Whatever he was discussing, he interrupted his speech, and he goes, "Ahem, ahem. I said, on the *right!*" Everyone turned and looked. He's glaring at Lawrence and me, because we had defied the tour guide, and we were looking out the left. We frankly weren't paying one bit of attention to what this guy was saying. We were talking with each other.

This was not, apparently, in tour guide school. This was a bad thing. So he corrected us. We had to turn and look out the right. I'm not sure what would happen to us, but we knew we were really out of line.

I sensed Lawrence was tightening up. I felt the hair standing up on the back of his neck as if to say, "I don't like this deal at all."

But we endured this trip. It was eighty miles. We get to Florence. We pull into this enormous courtyard, paved in beautiful old cobblestone blocks. Many, many busloads of people were parked there. They were on tours to go into this museum to see the statue of David and other beautiful works of art. Groups entered the museum at specific times. Repeatedly, our tour guide told us there was security at all of the doors, and we would not be permitted to leave the building. There were armed guards. They were very, very tight, security-wise, about this beautiful artwork. They had a right to protect the art of Italy.

We get off the bus in this big, massive courtyard. There are many different kinds of stores and sidewalk cafes. People mingle and shop, but the focus is this big museum. We get shoved like cattle toward this museum. It was neat that Lawrence and I were relatively tall compared to everybody else. I felt like I was looking down at the tops of everyone's heads. We did stand out a bit.

We're with this crew. They're shoving us. This obnoxious couple is in front of us. I'm thinking, "Of all the people that have to be in front of us, here is this miserable, full-of-hatred couple." But my goal is still to see this carved-marble statue. We're getting shoved in like cattle. Our tour guide's reiterating the fact about armed guards. We're getting closer to the entrance door. Other tour groups are there too. We're all being shuffled in exactly like cattle through a gate. I look around as we're getting ready to go through the door, and Lawrence isn't with me. I'm there by myself. I thought, "What happened to him?"

I can't move. I'm in the midst of this crowd. I get shoved right in with everybody else through the doors. I looked around, but I couldn't find Lawrence. I asked, but nobody knew where he was. He was there one minute and the next he was gone.

I went in and did look at the beautiful artwork. I did see the statue of David, and I was very pleased to see it. It was more beautiful than I could possibly have imagined. But as beautiful as that statue was, I enjoyed the company of Lawrence more. I thought, "How am I going to get out of this building?" The tour guide was adamant that we had to go to every single area this tour took us in this big building. I thought, "I've seen what I wanted to see. Now, I want out."

But they did have armed guards at all the exits. An armed guard was standing at this one door. He was very, very intense, and very official. He was alert and really doing his job. He's holding this rifle. He's holding it diagonally, pointed up in the air across his chest. I'm thinking, "How am I going to get out of here?"

Then I walked up to the door. The guy stands up and gets alert, as if to say, "Who is this woman coming toward me?" So I put my hand over my mouth and I held my stomach. I feigned I was going to get sick.

As rough and tough as this armed guard was, and as much as he knew about guns and weapons and protecting this beautiful artwork, he did not want some American tourist getting sick on him. He threw open the door and couldn't wait to let me get out. I ran through the door. I was thrilled. I had broken out. I broke out of this museum. I went into the courtyard.

I see at one of the sidewalk cafes a large crowd. Everybody's laughing and enjoying themselves. I know in the center of this crowd is Lawrence. Sure enough, there's Lawrence sitting there. There were American students and tourists, and others, sitting around. They're all telling their stories about how they got to Italy and what they're doing there. Some were studying art, some were traveling across Europe, and some elderly couples were fulfilling their lifelong dream to come to Italy. Everybody told their stories. Lawrence had bought a big block of cheese and bottles of wine. Everybody's sitting there drinking wine and eating cheese and bread. One after another would tear off chunks of this beautiful bread and tell their story. We had a ball. We sat there enjoying the fun.

The tour finally completes itself. I looked up and saw this tour guide standing there. He is fiercely angry with Lawrence and me because we broke the rules. We're not allowed to escape from the museum. He said to our group that people could board the bus now. The tour was boarding. We had to immediately finish what we were doing. We had to leave and get on the bus.

Lawrence had had enough of this tour guide. He had had enough of this obnoxious couple and some people on the tour. There was no way in hell he would get on this bus and travel eighty miles back. He told our guide, "Mister, I'll find my way back to Rome. Don't worry about me. You all just go on."

So they went on without us. We ended up in the company of a couple of young art students who took us back to Rome. That was a fun day, *and* I got to see the statue of David.

COMIC OPERA

Lawrence had a friend who was connected with the gambling casinos in Europe. This friend told us to look up a man while we were in Rome, a man named Shalini. Shalini was the money man for the gambling casinos. He really worked for the Mob. His job was to travel from country to country to different casinos to manipulate money. In those days, Yugoslavia had one of the biggest casinos and resorts in Europe.

It took a lot of skill to manipulate money from country to country. Most of these countries had rules. Italy was the worst about taking money in or out of Italy. This was during the time Sophia Loren was jailed because she was accused of taking money out of Italy. I forget how long she was in jail. They were very, very strict about this.

Shalini had a penthouse in the heart of Rome. He was married and had two children. His wife was so sweet. They were a beautiful couple, very handsome. I have a photograph of them. But they were the saddest people. The wife was so sad because they were literally prisoners of that city. This man was a very powerful man. But he was always watched by the authorities and officials of Rome and any place he went in Europe. Everybody knew what he was. He was the money man who transported money from place to place. He managed to get the Organization their money. He had a lot of people working for him. He was a fairly young guy to have so much power. He was an accountant, and he handled the books. He was very trusted. He had a tremendous amount of guts to do what he had to do.

They had this penthouse in the heart of Rome. They were literally prisoners. They had security guards. There were always threats against them, and threats about their children from kidnappers. They were marked. People wanted to get to them, because they knew there was a lot of money around. We contacted this couple because there was a common source that Lawrence knew. The man and the woman were thrilled to have an American couple there. They were American. They could talk to and entertain us, and not have the pressure of us wanting anything. We didn't want anything. We were just visitors in their city. He wanted to take us out to dinner.

The night we went out to dinner, we went to a comic opera. It was a comic opera house. Of course there's ten zillion opera places in Rome. Everybody sings opera. Everybody's an amateur opera singer.

We went to this place, and it was very popular. It was an old, beautiful building with a lot of carvings that reminded you of the old Mary Anderson and the Lowe's Theater, with all their ornate carvings and decorations on the walls. That's how this place was. It was very popular.

Six or eight of us went. Lawrence and I were the guests of the Shalinis. The place was packed. There was no place for us to sit.

The people at this comic opera place knew this man. Out of nowhere, they came with a table and chairs and sat us down in an area right in front of the stage of this comic opera. They shifted other people around.

They couldn't wait on this man enough. He had all the attention. He was a big spender, and he was an entertainer. He entertained people. He tipped. These people knew that. They set up a table in the center of this place. They pulled out the chairs and we sat down. We proceeded to watch this opera. The opera was really a lot of fun.

I looked up around the tops of the balconies of this theatre. It circled around two floors up. It was a fairly large place. I saw guards standing at virtually every single balcony. And they were looking down. They had guns. I said to Lawrence, "I wonder why the guards are all here." Lawrence kicked me on my leg under the table and told me to hush up.

But I don't pick up on what he's trying to tell me. So we're going on, and I start looking around. On the floor where we were seated, guards stood at all the entrances. People in uniform were everywhere. I thought,

"Golly, what is going on?" I said it again to Lawrence, "There must be somebody important here that they're looking out for. Look at all the security."

We found out later they were watching Shalini, our host. I had no idea. I thought how sad this woman was. She begged me to come up and visit her one more day while we were in Rome. But we didn't have time. She was a prisoner of this penthouse. She literally had nobody she could trust. She had hired help and people around her. But she was starved for attention from anyone who would talk to her woman to woman. I thought, "What good is all the money and the beautiful place that they lived in?" They couldn't enjoy anything. They lived in fear of being hurt and having their children kidnapped, and them being kidnapped.

When we left Rome, Lawrence and I were not married. We had passports with different names. When we boarded the plane with about 200 people from our tour, I was in one section and Lawrence was in another. We separated. He did this on purpose. He said, "I want you to stay in this part of the line, and I'll stay in another." He went all the way to the front.

The security came out to the airport. They surrounded this one airplane we were on. They took Lawrence out of the line. They took me out of the line. They took us to a little room and asked us lots and lots of questions. Their feeling was that, since we had met this man in Italy, he had given us something, or we had something or we had information we were taking out of the country, and they wanted to know what it was.

The one man who was questioning me was extremely hostile. He'd say, "Why did you come here?"

I said, "I came here because I'm on a tour."

He'd say, "Who did you come to see?"

I said, "I came to see the statue of David."

He said, "Well, why did you go here?" and "Why did you go there?" It became apparent that they'd kept a log on literally everything we did. Apparently when we first arrived in Rome, Lawrence put a phone call in to this man, and the authorities knew about this call. They must have had this man's phone tapped. So we had been watched the entire time we were in Rome. I had no idea of it. I was simply a tourist having a good time.

They finally gave up. There was nothing in our packages or luggage. There was nothing they could get from me or from Lawrence. They held up the plane for an hour-and-a-half, interrogating us. They put a special stamp on our passports. We boarded the plane again, and it was a while before I realized what the ramifications were. Shalini was eventually assassinated. Lawrence talked about him being killed. I've never seen or heard of his wife since.

VII. BUSINESS

Rooster Tail
Attempted Robbery
Shakedown
The Show Goes On
The Pig Roast
"How Was I?"
The Bondsmen
The Joy Ride
"I Will Not Testify Or Lie!"
"My Man Won!"

ROOSTER TAIL

The Rooster Tail Club was located at 421 West Chestnut Street. In the sixties and seventies, the club operators controlled whatever happened in their nightclubs. They did not depend on police departments or anybody else to settle their problems.

Lawrence never told anyone how he got the nickname "The Fox." But he did say it was connected to something he had done as a child. Everybody knew that he was foxlike in his manner. He was able to maneuver and arrange situations around him, especially in the operation of his club. He was foxlike.

If he had a customer who couldn't handle his liquor or had drunk too much, Fox knew what to do. Frequently he got people who came from other clubs, who already had too many drinks. Lawrence had his doormen trained to eyeball the situation, and they would send these people on home. They wouldn't let them in. Usually this could be assessed at the door. But sometimes the doorman couldn't tell that somebody had had too much to drink. They carried themselves well. They would come into the club and, as they would sit there, sometimes became obnoxious and out of line, and sometimes even violent.

Lawrence had two sons, Harvey and Larry, who worked the club. Sometimes I would come downstairs just to watch what was happening. We would spot a situation like this and, between the three of us, kind of guess how their daddy was going to handle the situation. Sometimes he would ask the individual if he would like a ride home or back to the hotel.

He would make sure he had cabdrivers out front. Bootsie Newman was one in particular. He would tell them, "Take this person back to the Brown," or "to the Seelbach," or wherever it was they were staying. "And make sure they get in safe." Or he would send them to their home. This worked out a lot of times. So he had no trouble with the customer, and the customer didn't get into any trouble.

But occasionally we ran into a person who was what we would call a "violent drunk." These cases were very hard to handle. A lot of times, Lawrence would say, "Come on, partner, let me buy you a drink." He could see they were getting more aggressive, more violent, and abusive in their language. The ball was rolling, and the person was quickly becoming out of control.

Lawrence walked the person to the back end of the club. They would stand up at the bar together. Lawrence would try to talk to him. First off, he would attempt to convince the man he'd had too much to drink and he needed to sleep it off. Sometimes that worked; sometimes it didn't. When it didn't, the person would say something like, "Well, I'm going to keep on drinking," or "I'm going to hurt you," or "I'm going to hurt the club." We knew then that Lawrence would order a drink for this person.

He would tell the bartender, "Buddy, fix him up a drink. What do you drink?" Whatever the guy drank, say, scotch and water, Lawrence had a signal. The bartender would put a drop of what we called "Shoo-Fly" in this individual's drink. Everybody would be signaled out of the way. The waitresses moved out of the way. Everybody backed up. They knew that this person, who was verbalizing how he was going to hurt Lawrence or hurt the club or hurt somebody or tear up the place, who had shown a tremendous potential for violence, would take a big drink of this drink.

Then, in a matter of seconds, he'd be to his knees. Whatever was in this mixture would cause him to get, instantly, stomach cramps, dysentery, violent vomiting. He would get hit like a ton of bricks. It was almost instantly as soon as it absorbed into his system.

The individual would go bolting out the door. Or he would run back to the restroom, and then bolt out the door. Either way, we would never hear from him again. That was a method by which Lawrence would prevent violence or abuse in his club. Lawrence wouldn't do this very often.

Occasionally, he had to revert to violence.

One time, Louisville hosted a big convention. It might have been a farmer's convention. We got a phone call from another club in the area downtown. Two men were systematically going from club to club causing a terrible amount of violence. They would get into the club and they would station themselves apart from one another. Then one or the other would start a fight. They'd pick up a chair or pick up a glass and throw it into a mirror. They'd end up tearing up the clubs.

These men had been in at least three clubs already that night. The operators in those days would forewarn one another. If Riney's bartender knew somebody was a problem, he'd pick up the phone and call Lawrence. He'd say, "Look, Fox, this is the description of these individuals. They got out of here." They'd forewarn each other and try to protect one another from these kinds of troublemakers.

These particular men were both ex-cons. They had gotten out of the penitentiary a few days prior. They had stumbled into Louisville in the midst of this convention and saw their opportunity. Big crowds were everywhere. The clubs were booming. People were out on the street. These guys could maneuver in and out of places and do their favorite thing — cause trouble.

Lawrence had a good description of these two men. He forewarned his crew and everyone what these men looked like. He told his people to be prepared for them.

When they arrived, Lawrence used a hand signal to let everyone know the men were there. One man sat down at the lower piano bar. The other man stationed himself exactly as another club operator had described it in his club. They didn't look at each other. They didn't acknowledge each other. Anybody who didn't know would think they were strangers.

They were sitting there getting ready. They were drinking. They were working their way up to causing trouble. Lawrence had a doorman named Jules, who was an enormous man. Jules went behind the one guy who was the follower, and Lawrence went to the man who was the leader. He took the guy by his arm and pulled out a gun and pointed it at him and told him he wasn't going to cause trouble in his place. To the other man he said, "You and your friend will get up and leave and will not come back."

This really made the man mad. His intention was to tear up another club. Now, before he had an opportunity to do it, he was being stopped. But he did get up because he had no way to defend himself against a gun. Lawrence and Jules walked these two men out. Out they went, and down the street.

It appeared that Lawrence had headed off at the pass a situation that could have been very bad.

Later that night, after the club closed, Lawrence and his son, Larry, and another man were restocking the beer. I was upstairs in the office making out the bank deposits and straightening out the money. We heard a loud, banging noise at the back door of the club. The door at the back of this club was a service door. It was wider than an average door and taller, because this door was used for carrying in and out cases of whiskey and beer. Lawrence had a metal bar across this door, to bolt it shut, plus he had dead bolts on it.

These men had returned. Lawrence had a peephole. He saw who they were. These two men had come back with pickhandles or baseball bats. They were banging the back door. They were bound and determined to get even with the man who stopped their joyride.

They swung the baseball bats and hit this door with all of their force trying to break it in. It looked like they were going to be successful. I came down the steps. Every time they'd bang on that door, the door vibrated in. It really looked like within a matter of minutes they'd have the door broken down. It was pretty frightening. Lawrence said to his son and to me, "Step back out of the way." He pulled out his gun and shot five or six times through the top of this door.

The noise stopped, instantly. He looked outside. He couldn't see anything. He couldn't see either of these men. So he unbolted the door, he unlocked it, and he opened it. The guys were crawling on their hands and knees through the darkness of the parking lot, the one guy yelling at the other, "Get out of here! That man's going to kill us!" They were running for their lives.

It looked like we got rid of these men *again*. Lawrence had done a lot of work around these buildings. He told his son, Larry, "Let's get rid of this door I shot through." They took the door off the hinges and brought up another door from the storeroom. They put the second door up to replace the door that was shot through. He went outside and picked up dirt and sand in his hands. He rubbed it on the new door to make it look like it had been used, as if it had been there for a while. Then they took the door with the bullet holes in it and slid it behind beer cases stacked in the beer room.

Then we went back to closing the club and doing the usual procedures we did. I finished the bank deposits. They finished restocking the liquor and the beer.

Before we left the club, we got a call from the police department. They're coming over because they have a complaint. About Lawrence. Lawrence said, "Fine. Come on over, Officers."

The police came in. They said they had a report that, for no reason at all, somebody shot at two men from the back end of our club. They had accused the Rooster Tail and the man who owned the club, of shooting at them. They didn't know Lawrence's name, so they didn't accuse him by name.

So Lawrence said, "Well, Officers, I know that these men mean well. But I don't know what they're talking about." He said, "You know, we've been busy tonight. You know, if people drink, sometimes they get confused about where they were. I did hear some noise. I think I heard some shooting. But I don't know where it came from."

The officers said, "Well, let's just look around." They went to the back end of the club. They were looking for bullet holes through the door that had been described to them. There were no bullet holes. The door was perfect. That dissipated that case.

ATTEMPTED ROBBERY

Another time, we had a particularly busy evening. Several conventions were in town. The place was very busy.

When Lawrence and I left the Rooster Tail, it was a little later than usual, probably about three in the morning. Lawrence would take the money and put it in a money sack. Usually he would tuck it into the side under his coat. He wasn't obvious about where he carried it. Generally he would take it home and make the deposit the following morning. Very rarely did he leave the money in the building. There was always a potential problem of being robbed.

He had a security system, The Sonic Guard, that we activated as we left the building. This company was wonderful. We'd call them and give them our code number, and they'd turn on the system. They could actually hear if anybody came in and broke into the building. They had caught a couple of burglars already. They caught one guy who came in through the attic and was all the way in the building. There was a constant concern about being robbed. Lawrence was a very cautious, careful man.

This particular night it was three-thirty in the morning. We were leaving, and I was not paying a lot of attention. He parked his car to the back of the building. It was dark except for lights around the building. But it was very dark. He would always open the door for me. As he opened the door, he said, "Get in the car. Be calm. We're going to be robbed."

I thought, "Oh my God!"

I get in the car and I sit down. I do what most people do in times when they fear being hurt; I started praying. Lawrence calmly went around to the other side of the car. He opened the door. He got in and sat down. He said, "In the parking lot, there's a car with two men in it. Their intention is to rob us. Now, don't get upset."

My heart had stopped. I thought, "Oh no — how are we going to get out of this jackpot?" We were pinned in. We were pulled into a spot in a little corral. If these people wanted to rob us, there was no way we could get out. They could just block us from behind. But they must not have realized that.

Lawrence eased the car back. I remember thinking, "My God, he's going so slow. Why doesn't he just move?" He just eased the car back like there was nothing wrong, as if he was not aware of anything. He pulled the car out of the parking lot. I looked in the mirror on the side of the car. Sure enough there was a vehicle sitting there and I could vaguely detect two figures in it.

So as Lawrence turned his car around, he angled it like he was pulling out of the parking lot. There was movement in the other vehicle. They were getting ready to get out of the car and come at us. But Lawrence put his foot on the gas and accelerated toward the exit of the parking lot, real fast.

These men turned on the motor of their car real quick, like they were going to chase us. As we reached the exit of the parking lot, instead of pulling out, Lawrence squealed his tires. He swerved to the right and turned all the way around. I was pitched forward in the car, he turned so fast. He drove his car as fast as he could straight toward these two potential robbers. They screeched to a stop and were totally stunned at the sudden change of events. Now, the person they were going to rob was suddenly coming at them.

The Fox stopped our car within a few inches of the other vehicle. I pulled myself up. When he had stopped so suddenly, I had plunged forward onto the floor in front of the seat. I pulled myself up in time to see Lawrence open the door of our car and leap out of the car. Everything happened so fast it was almost like a dream. He pulled his gun from his pocket. He shot up in the air above the robbers' car, several times. These men hit the floor of their car.

Then Lawrence got back in our car and we left. He said, and I'll always remember this, "Well, I don't think they'll try to rob us." And they didn't. Lawrence was so calm. That was the end of those guys.

Later on, Lawrence was a bondsman. He frequently got people out of jail for a lot of things. He helped catburglars and robbers. In this line of work, he ran into one of our parking-lot robbers years later. The guy told Lawrence, "You know, we were sure you were going to kill us that night." He said, "I tried to talk my friend into not robbing you." Lawrence had gotten this man out on bond on several occasions, and he knew this man. He said, "I knew, Mr. Detroy, that you would not tolerate being robbed. I tried to talk my friend out of robbing you, but he insisted. I am so grateful that you didn't shoot at us." He knew he could have. He could have shot both men, because what he did had happened so quickly and was so unexpected for them. The aggressors suddenly had the very person they were going after turn on them.

Lawrence didn't really hold much malice against these men. He understood they were robbers by trade. They had challenged him and he won. As far as he was concerned, that was the end of the issue.

The way Lawrence was brought up, in the era in which he was brought up, not unlike Frank, he had learned to live by his wits and his quick-thinking responses to situations around him. Lawrence's family included bootleggers and gamblers. As a child he observed them in dangerous and potentially violent situations. As a child he was brought up to know how to react and how to finagle out of these situations. It wasn't the sort of education offered at the University of Louisville.

SHAKEDOWN

When it became public that Lawrence and I were opening the Golden Fox Club in southern Indiana, we learned about how some people try to develop something and make a living. What happened is no doubt true in a lot of cases in little towns.

We had everything set up, finally, and we had to apply for the liquor license. That naturally publicized our intention. We had to go before the town board, which was very strict but very, very good to us. It was politics. Opening a business in a strange town means an element of politics. There was a nice police department. The police treated us very well the years that we were over there.

We had the lounge going, and we had bands for entertainment. It wasn't long before a girl came in off the street one morning. There was something about her I didn't like. I just did not like this girl. She had an attitude about her, an aura about her. I instantly felt she was a snake.

She said, "I need to talk to you." She was very, very intense. She made it sound like the most important thing in the world. "I'm going to help you," she says.

I said, "You're going to help me? You're going to help *me*? Is that what you're saying?"

"Yes, it's very important." She knew my name. She sought me out as soon as she came into our place. We were pretty busy. We had a busy lunch crowd. She said, "It's imperative I speak to you." So we went over and sat in a seat off to the side. It was her and myself. Lawrence wasn't there.

She proceeds to tell me that in order to maintain our liquor license in Clarksville, we had to pay a fee. I listened to her. "It's not that bad of a fee," she said. "It's just a little fee. You'll give me the money every week, and I'll see that the proper authorities get the money. You will not be bothered or harassed by the police department or the alcohol board or anybody else." She said, "You'll be totally protected. You won't have any trouble."

I'm sitting there listening to this little snake. I guess she sees me as a square. I said, "Oh, so you're going to help me keep my liquor license? And you're going to keep me from being hurt by other people, especially authorities, who may not approve of our liquor license. Is that what you're saying?"

"Oh, yes. And don't worry about it. This will be strictly confidential."

"Well, who is getting this money?"

"It's a representative of the police department."

"Oh, so you represent the Clarksville Police Department?"

"Yes."

"Well, I think that's just, God, that's just a wonderful position to be in. Who is this individual?"

She wouldn't say. But she was so confident, and I was just supposed to be so square.

I said, "Well, I think that's really good. Just sit here for a minute." I made our waitress give her some tea. I said, "Do you drink tea?"

She said, "Yeah."

"Well, have some tea. I'll be right back."

So I get on the phone and call Lawrence. Lawrence started laughing. He said, "Oh, brother!" So we decided I would go ahead and call the Chief of Police over there in Clarksville.

Then I went back, and I told the girl, "Honey, you just stay here. We'll get the Chief of Police over here. Then we'll sit down and we'll work out this payment schedule you're talking about."

Well, this girl just turned white as a ghost. She said, "What?! You called the police?"

"Well, sure! You represent them. And I wanted to meet Chief Detrich." He was the chief then. I really liked Chief Detrich, Ron. I said, "I think we need to work this all out. Let's get the details. I want to make sure we get the payment schedule correct." The girl was running over herself to get out of there.

"Well, I gotta go! I gotta go. Never mind! Never mind. You shouldn't have done that. You shouldn't have done that."

"Well, why not? You represent the Clarksville Police Department. I'm sure the Clarksville Police Department wants to do things correctly."

So she takes off. This kid took off. She flew out that door. She smoked the parking lot in her car.

Chief Detrich comes over and he said, "What's going on?"

I said, "Well, I think it's really nice. Your police department's asking me to pay a fee to operate this liquor license."

He got livid. He said, "What?! What are you talking about?"

I said, "Well...." Then I told him this story.

I never laid eyes on that girl again. We never had trouble with any authorities over there with the police department or the Alcohol Beverage Board. We had standard problems. But we were never harassed, and we never had to pay anybody. It was amazing. This girl was either a shakedown person, conniving with another person, or maybe she did represent somebody from the police department. But when I contacted the chief, it brought everything out in the open, and that ended the story.

The Show Goes On

We developed a nice place in Clarksville. Our lounge seated maybe 120 people, and we built another lounge/nightclub area that did special shows and seated about 350 people. We had banquet facilities. The place turned out to be humongous. Actually, it was not profitable for us in the long run. But at the time it was booming, and we hired a lot of bands.

This was an odd situation because Lawrence never was much on music, and I'm about as ignorant as can be. Anyway, it seemed like we were forever hiring bands for this place.

We had wonderful customers, and I would depend on them to tell me if a group was any good. I'd ask, "Are they any good?"

They'd say, "Yeah."

Whenever a band tried out, they'd have to try out in front of my customers. I'd take a reading. I could tell which band they would like, and which they wouldn't like. Naturally, I'd hire the one the customers like. That's the band that brings in the customers who spend the money that pays for the band.

We had really good luck. We hired one band every night in one room, and then another band for three or four nights in the other room. That's a lot of musicians. We had excellent luck. We had a reputation for being a club that was strictly operated.

One time, after we'd hired a host of different groups, we got talked into hiring one group we didn't really know much about. It was for a weekend.

When they came in, they didn't act right. They loaded in their equipment. They came in the back door of the lounge. There were some customers there in the afternoon who observed what was going on.

One of the customers came and got me and Lawrence. Our customer said the members of the band setting up were taking drugs out in the parking lot. The band was supposed to be real popular. The lead singer was like all the lead singers I ever met. They were legends in their own mind, very arrogant, with an "I'm a superstar" attitude, which used to crack me up.

Lawrence went to check it out. It was getting later into the evening. The band was due to start playing in a couple of hours. Lawrence went to them, and sure enough they were taking drugs out in the parking lot. He called a meeting with them. He said, "The only drugs that'll be sold on this premises, or used on this premises, will be alcohol, and I'll be the one selling it. I'll be the one making money. We don't need any other kind of drugs. That's a strict rule we have."

The lead singer was real arrogant. He was the leader of the band. He used foul language, and he said, "You have to just put up with us because there's no way you could get a band at this late date. You won't even have any entertainment if you fire us."

When the guy told Lawrence he couldn't fire them, that was just a real bad thing to do. Lawrence opened the door and he had his men take these guys' equipment and set it outside. He said, "All of it! Out!" He set it all out. He said, "And you all can go. Hit the road, and don't ever light in this door again."

The lead singer's yelling, "Well you'll be sorry. You won't have any band this weekend."

And Lawrence said, "If I have to, I'll hum 'Dixie' myself."

So he kicked out this band. In the lounge, we had a nice cross-section of customers. One man came up and he said, "I can play the guitar. I'm a singer." We knew him. We knew he did this part-time.

Then another guy came up and he said, "Well, I know how to play the drums. I have drums. We can get together a little combo."

That same night, our customers formed a band. It was probably one of the most fun weekends ever at the Golden Fox. The band was strictly customers, at the last minute. They entertained, and we just packed the customers in. Word spread that this band with no name was playing. But everybody knew the people. They were all customers. Some of them knew each other and some didn't. It turned out to be a lot of fun and very successful. It was a unique moment dealing with some of these entertainers.

THE PIG ROAST

The Golden Fox developed a really good clientele of customers. Sometimes I see the TV show "Cheers" and I can totally relate to the premise, with its variety of people from all walks of life who meet every afternoon for a drink. They know one another. That was the type of club we had.

We had secretaries, businessmen, truckdrivers, and every variety of person you can imagine. But it was a safe place. We wouldn't put up with anyone being abusive or hurting anybody. Both men and women felt secure coming into this club. They felt they could talk and have good conversation and laugh. They could watch television if there was a sporting event on.

One year, we had a customer with one arm. This guy was a real charismatic human being. I think he might have been born with one arm. He was a really nice guy. Everybody liked him. He was funnier than heck. He was a terrific storyteller. Usually when he came in the place, he always had something to say. Everybody was mesmerized by him and would listen to him. It was getting close to the Super Bowl. This guy wanted to talk about roasting pigs. He told me, "What you need to do is have a Super Bowl party and have a roasted pig."

I said, "I don't know how to roast a pig. I've never roasted a pig in my life."

I always have had a knack for delegation. I've always felt it was imperative to delegate. So I said, "I'll tell you what. Why don't I buy the pig, and you roast it? You do all the work." I said, "What we're going to do is, we'll have a Super Bowl party. I'll have the premises set up with television screens. I'll buy the pig. You get together the customers, and they can roast this pig and then serve it. I'm not going to even serve it. You guys are going to serve it. You're going to do everything for the Super Bowl party. We'll have a big party."

This was exciting. Almost anybody would like the idea of operating a nightclub. So I turned over the keys to this guy. We later nicknamed him, "one-armed pig man."

He lines up a crew. We get the pig. He brings this big roasting thing that somebody had. We put it out in front in the parking lot. It's going to be a two-day deal. He lines up volunteers. Our customers are all vying for position, to be able to sit out front with this pig roasting. This got to be a big thing. We actually had a list of names. So-and-So was going to be watching the pig from 2:00 to 2:30. So-and-So would be watching from 2:30 to 3:00. We had to put them in lots of five to six people, so everybody could officially say they helped roast this pig.

This deal got so big. It was really funny. It started out as a little idea, but it just kept growing and growing and growing. By the middle of the first day, our club was full of people waiting their turns to go roast this pig. The job was to stand outside and watch it turn on this spit.

Of course, the whole time they're roasting this pig, we're selling them drinks, food, and soft drinks, or whatever they want. It becomes this big party. By the day of the Super Bowl, there's tremendous excitement. Somebody sat with this pig while it was cooking, around the clock.

On the day of the Super Bowl, the place was absolutely packed in both rooms. I delegated different female customers and male customers. "You're in charge of serving the pig. You're in charge of picking up the plates. You're in charge of doing this. You're in charge of that." I gave them all jobs. All my regular employees had to do was sell drinks. The customers themselves were going to roast the pig, cut the pig, serve the pig, and clean up afterwards. This was the deal.

The parking lot was enormous. It went all the way back toward Value City. There were so many cars in the parking lot it looked like a circus. People were coming from everywhere. It was standing room only in the Golden Fox.

I was standing back behind the bar. I was trying to keep up with requests for drinks and food. We didn't have enough glasses. We were washing the glasses as fast as we could to keep up with the masses of people. Everybody's having a ball. I mean everybody. Everyone had a position. They all had jobs. All of my customers had jobs, and they got to delegate other people to do jobs. So this was a really neat thing.

At one point, I looked up. We had a coffee pot sitting over to the side. I looked up and there stood a little man. I'd never seen him before. He said, "Lady, what's going on here?"

I said, "Well, who are you?"

He said, "Well, I'm a salesman, and I'm staying at the Marriott. I was driving up Eastern Boulevard, and I saw all this activity. I thought, 'Well, I don't have anything to do. I'm going to come in.'"

I said, "Well, take the coffee pot over there and start pouring coffee." Some people were drinking coffee, and some people were drinking drinks.

"Oh, oh, oh, okay, Lady!" He grabbed the coffee pot. I'd never laid eyes on him before. But he proceeded to be in charge of the coffee pots. He kept the coffee going. He made new coffee. I gave him errands.

I said, "Get up and get those plates." We worked this poor little guy like a dog.

Everybody had a ball. The pig was wonderful. It tasted fantastic. There was so much laughing and carrying on. When we finished and everything was cleaned up, and we were closing down, this little guy was still there. He came to me. He said, "I don't know who you all are. I've never been in this city before. I've never been in a place like this. But, gosh! Can I come back next year when you do this?" This guy came back every year at Super Bowl time to spend Super Bowl day with us and pour coffee.

"How Was I?"

There was another entertainer named Gary Edwards. Gary Edwards is a singer. He's still around. He's very popular. He has a big following. He projects himself as an Elvis-type entertainer with the big, wide belts, the big sequins. He really is a very good singer. He had a good band. He played a lot at Flaherty's and other clubs.

He comes to Indiana, and he's going to book our larger club. The manager of the group said, "Whatever you do, do not compliment this Gary Edwards. He has a big head anyway and if you compliment him, his price goes up." It was an expensive band, and their contract required advertising. It was a big investment for us to hire this group.

But it turned out we did get a really good following. We had door coverage, and the place filled up. It was packed. The night the guy sang, he just sang his heart out. He was wonderful. He did everything any entertainer could possibly do. He sang his songs. He belted them out. He had choreography. The lighting and costumes were fantastic.

Lawrence and I are standing at the back of the club. Lawrence couldn't care less about music. His interest was making sure the register was ringing. This guy finished his set, and people were screaming and yelling. He impressed everybody. A lot of people in Indiana hadn't heard this guy before. They really liked him, and then he had his own following.

He came all the way to the back of the club where we were. He was sweating. He was patting his head with a scarf, *à la* Elvis. He asked, "How did I do?"

I looked at him and I went, "You were ... pretty good." I would not crack a smile.

That devastated this guy. He wailed, "I can't believe it. I sang my heart out. The people are screaming, and I'm just 'pretty good'?" He said, "You mean, you don't like me?"

I said, "No, no! No, no! We like you. Don't we, Lawrence?"

Lawrence said, "Yeah, yeah. You were okay."

So then anyway the guy left. The next set, he sang harder. He sang longer. He put his heart into it even more. He had the people *screaming*. They were just tearing the place down. He was absolutely wonderful. And again, he comes to us after he finishes the set, and he asked, "Well? What do you think?"

I said, "Well, I liked it a little bit better than the first set. Didn't you, Lawrence?"

We would not give this guy an inch. Not an inch. This poor guy was pathetic. The next time he booked our club, he had got it in his mind that he wasn't totally accepted in Indiana. He lowered his price. His manager told us it was the only time he ever knew that he lowered his price. It was because he was so upset to think we weren't falling all over him.

THE BONDSMEN

Lawrence served as a bondsman for many years. It was an interesting field. He acquired his bonding license under the line as far as being legal. He had had a conviction. He had a criminal history. He was able to pull some strings to get his bonding license. At the time, there were ten to fifteen other bondsmen in downtown Louisville. It was a booming, lucrative business.

To be successful in the bonding business, you had to really know the courts. You had to know your way around the police department. You had to have connections. Lawrence had developed over the years many, many different connections with all kinds of people. You had to have the clerks in the courthouse. They could make or break you. He had incredible rapport with these people.

Judge Colson was the criminal court judge. He had the power over the bondsmen. When Lawrence became a bondsman, he kept all the other bondsmen stirred up by needling them. He would make comments like, "Well, you've got a case here. Let me know, and I'll talk to my man." That signified to these other bondsmen that he had these connections.

Lawrence would needle the bondsmen. Then they would come to the judge's office. They would say Lawrence said this and Lawrence said that. It was a constant hassle for Judge Colson because Lawrence would stir up all these other men, and then he would go make the bonds and make the money, while they argued among themselves, all upset and aggravated over something that he had said to them.

Finally, Judge Colson said, "I've had enough." He said, "I've heard from every one of those men. They're like a bunch of little kids. They infuriate me." And he announced, "I've called a meeting of all the bondsmen into my courtroom." They all arrived at the appointed hour. Lawrence sat up front. All of the men didn't know what would happen. The judge had the power to take them off the board, so they could not make a bond. Of course, if a bondsman couldn't make a bond, he couldn't make money. Judge Colson had tremendous power over these men.

He sat up there on the bench. He took the gavel. He pounded it. He screamed and yelled. He told them, "I do not want to hear one more story. I do not want to hear one more conversation. There will be no more complaints about Lawrence Detroy. Lawrence Detroy is not in my pocket. He does not control my decisions! He has nothing to do with my decisions. You are not to listen anymore to him making those cracks.

"Any decision I make is made because I have weighed up the situation. I make my decisions on my own! There is no outside interference and no outside suggestions when I decide!"

Everybody in the courtroom, all the bondsmen, sat there in stony silence. Lawrence was sitting up front. He had his arms crossed across his chest. He was listening just as intently as everyone else. The whole thing was about him.

Judge Colson wanted to make sure his message got across. He said, "Does anyone have any comments to make?"

Silence. Then finally Lawrence raised his hand real slow. He said, "Yeah, Judge, I want to ask you something."

Judge Colson had no idea what Lawrence was up to. He said, "What, Lawrence?"

Lawrence said, "Well, let me get it straight. Do you want me to stop lying to the other bondsmen? Or do you want them to stop believing me?" Everybody fell out laughing. It killed the whole purpose of Judge Colson's meeting that day. But even the judge laughed uproariously.

THE JOY RIDE

One of the judges in the criminal court despised Lawrence. He never understood how Lawrence managed to finagle and get things done in spite of him. He was jealous.

A friend of Lawrence's, one of the Allens, Rufus Allen's little brother, got in trouble. He was just a kid, maybe fifteen, sixteen years old. He was sitting in front of his house when a friend drove up in a car and offered him a ride.

So they get in the car. The Allen boy asked the kid, "Where'd you get the car?"

The kid said, "Oh, I stole it."

Right away, the Allen kid said, "Let me out." So the Allen boy and the other passenger got out on the very corner where they were picked up just across the street.

The police catch the kid joyriding and he says, "Well, I, well, there were two others with me." The cops head out after the two boys he's named. One was the Allen boy. Rufus Allen and Lawrence Detroy were very good friends. Rufus was quite a character. He had a babyface. The police arrest the Allen boy.

So Rufus went to Lawrence and said, "Help my little brother. They're talking about putting him in a detention home." And he said, "My brother did make a mistake, but he realized it, and got out. It really doesn't justify being hurt."

So Lawrence goes with the Allens to the courtroom. There sits this judge who was Lawrence's archenemy. There's a social worker in the courtroom. She was dating the judge. The social worker's advising them how this kid's never been in trouble before. This kid had no record of being in trouble.

The judge said, "What exactly do you have to do with this, Mr. Detroy?"

Lawrence said, "Well, Judge, I'm the friend of the family." He said, "This boy's a good boy. He's never been in trouble. He was gettin' ready to sign up to go into service." That meant it was imperative he not have any marks on his record.

The judge said, "Well, Mr. Detroy, you're his friend. And you're not a lawyer, is that correct? Are you an attorney?"

"No. I'm just a friend of the family."

"This boy is going to spend time in a detention home," the judge announced. He intended to give as great a punishment as the boy could get and he was allowed to impose under the law. Then the judge bawled Lawrence out. He said, "You think you can come and go in the courts. You think the clerks and judges work for you. Well, this judge doesn't work for you. You'll see how that is!" Lawrence nodded his head affirmatively, and then left.

But Lawrence meets the judge out in Congress Alley. The judge said, "I fixed you, didn't I?"

Lawrence said, "That kid will not spend one night in the detention home."

They had a few more little words, and the judge said, "Well, he will."

Lawrence and a prosecutor named Higgins went immediately to another judge who was a step above this guy, and they told him what happened. The higher judge heard how this other judge was very jealous and vindictive. He said, "Well, that's no way to handle it. I won't let that go on."

The judge and prosecutor Higgins wrote a letter. It said, "Release the boy forthwith," and so forth. They sent Lawrence with two policemen out to the detention home to pick up the boy.

So Lawrence goes out there. He says to the man at the detention home, "I'm here to pick up the Allen boy. Here's the paper the judge gave me."

But the guy said, "I'm not releasing the boy." He said judge so-and-so said not to release him no matter what.

"You're not releasing him?"

"No."

"You understand what I have here."

"Nope, not going to release him. He said you're no good, and not to release Allen."

Lawrence turns around and goes back downtown. He goes into Higgins' office. He says, "They said that you were a no good such-and-such. They said they don't have to do what you suggested that they do." Then Higgins blew.

Then he sent Lawrence back to the detention home with two more policemen. But this time they had a warrant for that guy's arrest. They show him the warrant. He says, "You can't arrest me."

Lawrence said, "You have defied a court's order. Apparently you seem to think you're above the court system. It doesn't look that way. I suggest you get someone to watch this desk."

Then they turn around and take the guy downtown. They take him straight to the higher judge who issued the warrant. The judge dressed him down. He said, "Just where do you think you have the power to overrule an order? This court gave an order to release that young man. Now, *you* will serve time in jail, and you will find out what it's like to be punished. Meanwhile, that young man is going to be released."

The guy pleaded, "Please, please, please." He started begging. "Please, don't arrest me. Please. I'm sorry. Judge So-and-So called me. He told me no matter what, if Detroy arrived, do not give him this kid."

After all that, Lawrence and the two policemen went back, and the boy was released to them. Then Lawrence made a point to go downtown into the first judge's chambers. He waved at the judge who'd been so mean, pointed to the boy, and called out, "Not one night!"

"I Will Not Testify Or Lie!"

The Frank Sinatra movie portrays Robert Kennedy the way Lawrence felt Kennedy really was. It didn't treat him as a hero who was assassinated and a wonderful man.

Lawrence was involved in an episode with the FBI and Robert Kennedy. When Attorney General Kennedy investigated Jimmy Hoffa and wanted to take him to trial, he needed a federal court district where the judge would really be hard. The judge in the Western District of Kentucky was one of the roughest. He was a hanging judge, and that's where Kennedy wanted to hold the trial.

Lawrence was the bondsman who handled the Teamsters' account. Essentially that meant that when truckdrivers had traffic problems or drinking problems, or worse, Lawrence's bonding company would post the bond and handle the case. He had a very lucrative working arrangement with the Teamsters.

Lawrence met Jimmy Hoffa only once. That was at some function. It was just shaking hands. He never really spoke to the man. But he did handle the majority of the Teamsters' business. The Teamsters needed a company they could rely on, that would produce when their drivers got in trouble, or had problems in other states. They had bondsmen all over the country to handle their business. Lawrence wasn't the only one.

One day, Lawrence was in court. His secretary Kathy was in the office. The FBI came in and said, "We want to speak to Lawrence Detroy." Lawrence was on his way back. Kathy didn't know what was wrong. The agents were not real friendly. Lawrence came in. It was obvious who the visitors were.

Lawrence said, "What can I do for you all?"

They said, "We want you to testify against Jimmy Hoffa when we have a trial here in the Kentucky district."

"Oh, really? Testify to what?"

"Well, you know, testify that he gave you money on the side and had you do things for the company and that sort of thing, crooked."

Lawrence said, "He never did do that." He said, "We had an honorable contract where I represented, as a bonding company, the Teamsters. Nobody asked me to ever do anything illegal. Everyone has a right to a bond." He added, "I handle other companies, too."

One agent said, "But we want to make a case in Kentucky."

"No. You're wanting me to lie. I won't do it."

The agents got upset with him. They knew Lawrence had a person run out on a bond that was going to cost him ten thousand or twenty thousand dollars. It was a big number. When a defendant runs out, the bondsman has to pay the whole bond. Lawrence was having difficulty tracking this individual down, and the FBI knew about it. One agent said, "We can get this bond to be forgiven. You should help us. If you don't cooperate, you're going to have to pay that bond yourself."

Lawrence blew up. He threw them out of his office. He said, "I'll pay the bond. That was my mistake. I made the mistake of making that bond for that individual. It has nothing to do with Robert Kennedy or you all. I will not testify against Jimmy Hoffa. I'll be your worst witness on the stand, so you'd better find another district."

So he threw them out. The next day, the agents came back. They informed him he would be, thereafter, on their list. The FBI would watch him. He said, "That's fine. I'm sure, off and on over the years, you all have followed me anyway."

He said, "I don't like your techniques. I don't like what you're trying to do. You're trying to frame a man instead of building a legitimate case. You're doing the very thing that you're saying he's done. You all are worse! I won't be a party. I won't have a thing to do with it. Whatever you do to me, I'll just take it." And he pitched them out again.

The FBI finally tried its case against Hoffa in Tennessee, which was the next toughest district. Lawrence always said Robert Kennedy was absolutely no good and that he was a vicious, ruthless man, even though it was not a popular thing to say or not a popular thing to go along with. Robert Kennedy was so glorified after Jack Kennedy died. The ironic thing was, Lawrence really liked Jack Kennedy. He admired him and respected him, but he always felt that his little brother was probably his worst enemy — that he made things worse for Jack Kennedy.

Lawrence went to his grave never changing his opinion about Robert Kennedy. "I don't care how many statues or monuments they put up for the guy," he said, "the guy was *no good*."

"My Man Won!"

Lawrence had his bonding office right by the courthouse. Every day, Judge Colson would have to walk past the office. Colson was a Republican who had a favorite candidate running for office.

Judge Colson and Lawrence had a love-hate relationship. Lawrence supported the Democrat running against Colson's friend. So Lawrence put an enormous picture of the Democrat candidate in the window of his office. It was the prime location because the office was right there by the courthouse.

Colson would pass by every day on his way to and from court. He would stop in and say hello to the Fox. He liked Lawrence, and he'd make a crack about him having a picture of the candidate running for office. Lawrence would say, "He's gonna win! What do you mean? He's my friend, and he's gonna win!" They would banter about this guy because Colson was for the Republican and Lawrence had the Democrat in the window.

The night of the election, it became apparent that the Democrat was going to fail miserably. Lawrence went to his office and took the big photograph down. This man he'd been needling Judge Colson about for weeks and weeks and weeks had lost. Lawrence got a little newspaper clipping of the fellow who was winning and put it in the window.

The next day Judge Colson comes by. He says, "Well, your man got beat."

Lawrence says, "What do you mean? My man won! I've got a picture in the window!"

Colson got a big kick out of that.

VIII. KIDS

Edwina's Introduction
Dates with Edwina
The Flood Line
Adventures with the Kids
Buildings Don't Fall Out of the Sky
Colin's Pierced Ear
Best Friends
Display Rack
Future Daughter-in-Law

Edwina's Introduction

When Lawrence and I first got married, my twin brother Buzz had also been married for a couple of years. He lived in New Jersey. He married a beautiful Irish girl named Leontia, a red-headed Irish girl. They had a baby while they were living in New Jersey.

Buzz decided to move back to Louisville. He and Leontia came to Louisville with their little baby girl named Edwina. Edwina must have been six months old at the time. I was looking forward to seeing the baby for the first time. We had a dinner at our house for my brother and my sister-in-law and their little baby.

Leontia jabbers all the time. I just love her dearly. She's trying to forewarn us that this child has a terrible dependency upon her. The child would not go to anybody. The minute her mother would leave her, she'd have terrible separation anxiety. She'd cry and scream. She was very, very dependent upon her mother. She did not want anyone to pick her up. Nobody could handle this baby but Leontia. She wanted to let us know because she didn't want our feelings to get hurt when we met this baby the first time. I said, "Oh, that's okay."

Lawrence never really had much opportunity to be around children during his earlier years. When he was raising his boys, he was working around the clock in the bonding business. He had a beautiful niece, Sarah, but they moved out of town. So he really wasn't around little children that much. I didn't know how he was going to respond.

Buzz and Leontia came over. Leontia's holding this beautiful little girl in this cute little pinafore. The little girl had blonde, short hair with curls that were little tufts of curls on the nape of her neck. *God,* she was a beautiful child. Leontia was holding her in her arms. She's trying to forewarn us again, to remind us that Edwina would not go to anybody.

Edwina was *just* a baby. She turned and looked at Lawrence, and Lawrence looked at her. She stuck both of her arms out and reached for Lawrence to take her. Leontia's mouth fell open. She couldn't believe it. This child never went to anybody. The baby just immediately smiled real big as if to say, "Oh, you're okay."

Lawrence took that baby. And from that time on, that little girl had Lawrence's heart. As she grew bigger, Edwina would come and stay with us a lot. She would stay for a couple of nights, usually every week. We always had adventures and did things with her.

Lawrence was not allowed to read stories to her because he didn't read the way I did. So he created stories for her. Then later on, he'd create stories for her brothers. He gave them stories. He made up a story for Edwina that had a character in it who was a honey bear. This honey bear went everywhere. Of course, the honey bear had a little friend named Edwina.

DATES WITH EDWINA

Edwina and Lawrence had such rapport. It was funny to see this businessman with this little girl. Every day during the week, Lawrence would meet his friends Frank Haddad, Larry Higgins, Harry Ammons, Morris Brown, and a variety of businessmen, for lunch at Stouffer's. It would always be Frank and Lawrence with the different groups of men.

But about once every two weeks, Lawrence would have a date with his little niece, Edwina. When Edwina was around three or so, he would go pick her up. She would be dressed in a little pinafore with her tights and her patent shoes and her hair combed, real cute. And he would take her to Stouffer's for lunch.

Edwina was always an independent child. She did not like being carried. When she was able to walk, she wanted to walk. She did not like to be carried. They would come in Stouffer's. He'd park in the back. They'd walk down this long corridor. This little girl with her patent shoes and her tights and this man, holding her hand. They would take their time.

They'd walk down the hallway. They'd stop and speak to the lifeguard at the swimming pool, the man in the barber shop, the manicurist, the catering office people. They'd visit with everyone. Lawrence would take his time. Edwina would chat with the gift shop lady. They would walk down this long hallway, which would take a good twenty minutes. Normally it would take four or five minutes to get down the hallway. But they stopped to talk to everybody and greeted everyone.

Then they would come to the dining room. The hostess would seat them at a table by themselves. Edwina, the little girl, would be put in a booster chair. Lawrence would sit across the way. And they would sit there and have a date. They would talk. Lawrence really enjoyed Edwina. I was a dietitian there. I would stand back behind a corner and watch them. They would be engaged in very deep conversation. He listened to what this little girl would say to him, and she listened to her Uncle Lawrence.

Some of the businessmen who would eat lunch with him didn't understand. Inevitably, one would come up and say, "Well, Lawrence...." He would want to pull up a chair and sit down.

Lawrence would tell them, "I'm sorry, fellas. Y'all have to sit over there. I'm having lunch with my niece." One of the men, Larry Higgins, would get furious.

This would baffle these other men. They'd just get aggravated to think that Lawrence wouldn't let them sit down at the table. But he was serious. It was not the time for him to shoot the breeze with the men. It was a time for him to sit and talk to his little niece and get to know her. This relationship developed into a beautiful relationship. Uncle Lawrence and Edwina had many a meal together. They had many a dinner, as the years went on, before he died. Edwina treasures them all.

Lawrence did the same thing with his nephews Liam and Colin. Lawrence finally was able to have the opportunity to be involved with children as he got older in life. He loved that. He loved to interact with these kids. He liked to be involved with what they were doing. He loved to talk to them and listen to them. He always encouraged them to talk to him. He would sit and listen.

It's something we don't do with children today. We do not involve them. We do not give them the opportunity to express their feelings to us. And then we wonder why kids won't listen when we want to talk.

THE FLOOD LINE

Lawrence would do things with Liam and Colin. One time it flooded downtown, and it was going to flood River Road. He went and picked up Colin and Liam. They were little boys at the time. He took them down to River Road. He showed them where the water line was. He said to them, "Now, tomorrow the water's going to crest." He told them the water was going to do this and that and the other. He said, "We're going to follow this." He knew it was going to take about a week for the water to rise and crest and go back. He wanted these boys to see this.

So, every day for a week, he took those kids down to the same spot on River Road and showed them the differences. It finally got to the point where they couldn't go. It flooded. They could only get so far. But he would take the time to do things like that with the kids. They would study this, something that the rest of us take for granted.

ADVENTURES WITH THE KIDS

Another thing Lawrence would do with the kids was to go on a Sunday drive. These kids would call it an adventure. He'd go pick them up. He'd say, "Let's go take a ride." They never knew where they were going to go. But they always knew it would end up an adventure.

Buildings Don't Fall Out of the Sky

When the big contractors were building the LG&E building downtown on Third Street, at Third and Main, Lawrence would pick up little Liam and Colin and take them downtown. There was a chain-link fence around this building. The earth movers had dug an enormous, deep, deep basement to this building.

Lawrence introduced himself to the foreman of the job. He said, "My name's Lawrence Detroy. These are my two nephews. They're little boys. They've never seen a building built before. Do you mind if we come down and just watch you as you progress with this building?" The foreman was surprised and pleased that somebody was interested in what he was doing.

So every week, a couple of times a week, Lawrence would pick up those little boys. He'd drive them downtown. They'd park the car. They'd get out. The foreman would come over, and he'd explain whatever problems they were having. For instance, in the beginning, water kept seeping into this big hole that they dug. They had to dig extra trenches and make different types of preparation to prepare the basement of this building. Those boys observed the equipment and all of the work that went into creating this building.

Somebody asked Lawrence, "Why are you doing that with these kids? That's a lot of trouble."

Lawrence said, "It isn't any trouble. Kids need to know that buildings don't fall out of the sky. They need to know how they're built!"

This was Lawrence's way of trying to teach these kids that everything, that everybody, has a purpose. Things do take hard work to create. A beautiful building doesn't just pop up. It took men, groups of men, using all kinds of tools, to build this building. It took tons of equipment. These kids got to observe this. They were involved in a way. The foreman always made a point to explain to these kids what was going on.

COLIN'S PIERCED EAR

These kids went to Holy Trinity, a Catholic school. In the beginning of each school year, frequently Lawrence and I would be the ones to take them to school and pick them up. Things would come up. Sometimes they took the bus. But usually they had a ride, and a lot of times we would take them.

Lawrence would use the time driving the kids to subtly give them lectures and advice. He would sound them down and find out what was going on in their lives. Whatever was happening.

Lawrence and I were both real adamant about one thing. Every year, at the beginning of the school year, when we would take the kids to school, they'd say, "Yes, we know. If there's a new kid in school...."

We would say, "Now, if there's a new child at school, or somebody that's different at school, make a point to be nice to that kid. Don't let anybody pick on the child or bully the child. You be the leader. You welcome the person and show kindness." Lawrence would give this lecture to the kids every time. They knew it frontwards and backwards, and that he was right.

I don't think Colin or Liam or Edwina ever participated in shunning anybody, or picking on anybody. They always made it a point to try to include the outsider. We're all exposed to new people at different times. Sometimes, we do tend to shun people. It's a bad habit that we have as a society. But Lawrence always said this to the kids. So they learned to practice that, to show consideration for others.

When Colin was thirteen, the year before Lawrence died, he stayed with us a lot. Colin and Lawrence had terrific rapport with one another. They reminded me of, and I would say it to people, "They're like two little old men on a park bench." They understood each other. I would go to work at night. Colin would spend the night. Lawrence would take him to school and pick him up. I'd say to them, "Don't tell me what you two do when I'm not here." They cooked. Lord knows what all they prepared in that kitchen. I didn't want to know.

They really had good rapport. Colin was very protective of his Uncle Lawrence. Colin would get up in the morning before they would go to school to fix him biscuits and make sure that he had something to eat. This little boy did this for his uncle.

Lawrence was old-fashioned in his manner. He had old-fashioned beliefs. One of the things that he didn't like was to see earrings in boys' ears. I think most men of his era felt the same way. He would make a comment to Colin about this. "I don't like those earrings! Can't stand to see a kid with an earring in his ear!" Colin would listen to him, and go on about his business.

Colin and his best friend had made both of their mothers promise that if they both stayed on the honor roll at Holy Trinity, then they could get one wish that they wanted. The wish would be granted. Both these women agreed to this without knowing what the wish was. I tried to forewarn Leontia. I said, "*Please*, don't ever make a deal with a kid unless you know what he's talking about!" But anyway, they agreed.

Colin did stay on the honor roll. He maintained his grades. At the end of the school year, he presented his wish. His wish, along with Reed's, was to get their ears pierced. So their mothers relented.

Leontia calls me and asks, "What do you think Uncle Lawrence is going to say?"

I said, "I don't know." I only knew he always made cracks that he didn't like earrings in boys' ears. So, I said, "But that's your decision. I cannot make that decision for you."

Then little Colin asked me. I said, "It's your decision, Colin. You have to do what you think is right. I'm not involved." So Colin and his best friend each had one ear pierced. Then each had that little stud put in his ear when it was first pierced. Colin came over to our house to spend the night. He's got this newly pierced ear with the stud in it that he had to turn and put alcohol on. It's a lot of work, getting a pierced ear. I don't think the boys really knew how much work it was going to be.

But Colin loved his Uncle Lawrence. He didn't want to upset his Uncle Lawrence. He didn't know how to get around making him mad about the pierced ear. So he took a Band-Aid and covered the stud on his ear.

Colin stayed with us for three days. He would get up in the morning. He'd come down to the kitchen table. He loved to cook. So we would cook breakfast, and we would sit there and eat. He'd have this Band-Aid over his ear. For three days, Lawrence would sit at the table, and they would talk about everything. He would never make a comment about Colin's ear. And it got to Colin. It got to this little boy, because he was hiding the fact that he'd had his ear pierced.

Finally, he said to me, "I've gotta tell Uncle Lawrence."

I said, "It's up to you, Colin. It's your decision."

So he tells his Uncle Lawrence. "Uncle Lawrence, I have something to show you." He removed the Band-Aid off his ear and showed the stud. The earring stud. Colin was scared. He didn't want to disappoint his Uncle Lawrence. Yet he did something that all kids do, something with their appearance. It was a challenge, especially at that age. It was the "in" thing to do for the kids. On the other hand, he didn't want to disappoint his Uncle Lawrence. He didn't want his Uncle Lawrence to be mad at him.

Lawrence looked at him and said, "Well, thank God, Colin!" He said, "I thought something was festering under there!" He did not belittle Colin. He did not say a thing about not approving of the earring. He accepted the fact that Colin did pierce his ear. It was Colin's decision. Lawrence never made a big deal out of it. The easy thing to do would be to start carrying on about it. "Well, that looks terrible," and, "Boys shouldn't have pierced ears!" But Lawrence didn't. He cooled his heels on it.

From that point on, when Lawrence would take Colin to school, they followed a routine. A student was not allowed to wear an earring in his or her ear in the Catholic school. So Colin would wear his earring to the school. Then he would take it out. When he got up into the schoolyard, he would hand his Uncle Lawrence the earring. He'd say, "Keep an eye on it!"

Lawrence would kid him. "Colin, can I borrow your earring while you're in school?" He would needle him about this earring.

When Lawrence died, little Colin went to the casket. One of Colin's earrings was a shamrock. He took the shamrock earring, and he stuck it in the lapel of Lawrence's suit. He said, "Yes, you can have it." This was a little boy's way of saying goodbye to his Uncle Lawrence and leaving something in the casket with his Uncle Lawrence that was between the two of them.

BEST FRIENDS

When Colin was eleven years old, his school, Holy Trinity, celebrated a day called Friendship Day. On that day each student invited his very best friend to school to introduce them to the entire class. Each student signed and wrote a little paper about what friendship meant to them.

The *Courier-Journal* newspaper has a section they call the Neighborhood Section, in which a photographer and a reporter report on interesting events around the community and Kentucky. They just pick them out. They decide to cover it. They feature little fairs or something that's going on in some neighborhood.

This particular day, Friendship Day, the *Courier-Journal* reporter and photographer went to Holy Trinity to record these children celebrating friendship. Colin invited his Uncle Lawrence. Most students invited kids or people their age. But Colin invited his Uncle Lawrence.

Later the photographer called me, and she said, "I was amazed at watching this man with this little boy. You could see they had such a rapport." She kept taking photographs of them. She sent me a sheet of all the photographs she took. There must have been fifteen or twenty photographs of Lawrence interacting with this little boy. She said most of the kids really didn't know what to say. They didn't have much to say when they got up to talk about and introduce the person they brought. But, she said, when Colin got up, he was very straightforward. He spoke up very loud, and confidently. He said, "This is Uncle Lawrence. This is my best friend. He's my best friend because I could tell him anything. We can talk about anything, and it is between the two of us."

The teacher said to me later, "I listened to this little boy describe this relationship with his uncle and I thought, 'God! *I'd* like to have a friend like that!'"

The photographer told me, "I spoke to your husband, and I want you to verify this with me and tell me if it's true." She said, "He does not have a business now?"

I said, "No, he's retired."

She said, "Does he actually have a pager that is for those kids?"

"Yeah, he does." I said, "He really does." That surprised her.

She said, "You mean to tell me that if any of those children need him, all they have to do is page him?"

"That's right. They page him, and he returns the call every time."

DISPLAY RACK

Lawrence managed to take each one of them — Liam, Edwina, and Colin, and even Morgan, fishing. He taught them how to fish. When Liam was little, he was fascinated with building things. Lawrence got a model airplane, and Liam and little Larry and Colin sat at the kitchen table to work on it. It was one of those balsa wood kits that you had to cut out with a knife. They sat at the table and built these little airplanes.

Lawrence was always fascinated with Liam's ability to build. One time Lawrence and another man operated a booth at the fairgrounds. They were going to sell T-shirts. They had cubicle display cases they were going to build to display these shirts in. Liam was young. He might have been twelve or thirteen. And Lawrence would take the kids with him when he did things like this.

He took Liam up to the fairgrounds. They were setting up. It was in one of those big buildings at the Kentucky State Fair where they had all these displays. They're trying to set it up. These cubicles or cases had been delivered. This cluster of men could not figure out to save their soul how to put these things together. It was so complicated. The directions said, "A to B and B to C," and so on. There were pieces everywhere. Nobody could figure out anything.

Lawrence knew that Liam could take a diagram and look at it and put something together just like that. It was Legos to Liam. Nothing had ever fazed Liam about how something was put together and created.

Lawrence told the men, "Look, y'all. We're going to be here all day long unless somebody figures out how to put it together." He handed the directions to little Liam. In a matter of minutes, this kid showed them how to assemble the display cases they'd been fumbling and bumbling with for hours.

Lawrence was involved with these children. He made things interesting for the kids. He made it a learning time. Everything combined an adventure and a learning experience. He tried to instill that combination into those children.

FUTURE DAUGHTER-IN-LAW

Lawrence's two sons, Larry and Harvey, really loved their father. Lawrence loved them so much. He worried about them all the time and was so proud of both of them. Harvey lived with Lawrence when he was going to college. They had wonderful rapport, Harvey and Lawrence, and Larry and Lawrence also.

Harvey was dating a lot of different ladies. He was quite popular. He met a woman named Billie. Billie Schott. Billie had been married for a short period as a teenager. She had a child, and then a divorce. She really was a single parent, with her daughter. The little girl's name was Amy.

Harvey started dating Billie. He really liked her. Billie is not only a beautiful woman. She's very smart. She's a very compassionate and giving person. When Lawrence met Billie, he thought she was the greatest woman in the world for Harvey. Then he met little Amy, just a toddler at the time.

We marked time from this meeting. Lawrence adored this little girl. Whenever Harvey and Billie and Lawrence and I would have a dinner or do something, Lawrence would introduce Billie as his future daughter-in-law. Harvey sometimes would look at his father like he could kill him. That was his decision, not his father's.

But Lawrence fell in love with Billie and Amy. He got such joy out of Amy. He would take her places. He would take them to the zoo. We would go to the Derby parade. So we'd have Amy and Billie and little Edwina, and Sarah, when she'd come to town. All the kids would be together. We would get a special spot for the Derby parade outside Stouffer's. I've got photographs of us watching the parade going by. Lawrence absolutely fell in love with Amy.

Finally, Harvey and Billie decided to get married. When they got married, Lawrence was in seventh heaven. Now, he had a grandchild he absolutely adored. He was so proud of Amy. Amy was a bright child, and a very easy child to be around. She was a total delight. And sweet. Lawrence was just in seventh heaven.

There were a couple of extremely proud moments for Lawrence in regard to Amy. One was when she graduated from college, from Centre. Lawrence was thrilled. Just absolutely thrilled that Amy did as well as she did and graduated from Centre. We went to that graduation. There was not a person in the room prouder than Lawrence Detroy of his granddaughter Amy.

The other thing that Amy, when she turned thirteen, did was to act on her decision to change her name. She changed her last name from her father's name to Detroy. It was her idea. It was not Billie's or Harvey's idea. It was strictly Amy's idea. And when they told Lawrence that Amy wanted to change her name, he was so proud. He asked her why.

She said, "Because Harvey's been more a father to me than my real father, and I want his name. I love him. I want the Detroy name." That was a strong act for a thirteen-year-old child. Generally, a teenager's not in that frame of mind to start with. But Amy appreciated the love and the care that she got from her dad, Harvey, and from Lawrence. She just said, "Let's go to court and officially make my name Detroy."

The last week that Lawrence was alive, it became obvious he was slipping very quickly. I tried to allow him to touch all the people he loved. But he hated to have people hovering about him. He didn't want anyone to be standing over his bed when he was sick.

But I plotted with Billie. I said, "Billie, I think it's imperative that we get Harvey with his daddy. But we've got to do it in a way that it doesn't look like Lawrence is on his deathbed."

She said, "Well, what can we do?"

I said, "Let me make arrangements to get him to your house."

The problem was Lawrence was so weak it was difficult to even get him ready to go any place. Or for him even to have staying power once he was ready. Even a short walk was very difficult.

On a Sunday, Billie and Harvey were going to church. She had a cordless phone. She said, "I'll keep my phone in my purse. You ring me when you think you're going to be able to get to the house."

I knew it would take me the greatest part of the morning to encourage Lawrence to get up and move about. I talked to him about it. I said, "Why don't we ride over and see Harvey?"

"Yeah, I'd like to do that," he said. "I'd like to see Harvey." He loved Harvey and always worried about him. "I want to check on him and make sure he's okay."

I went, "Okay." It took me all morning. I fixed Lawrence breakfast. He got dressed. Everything was very difficult — putting shoes on, everything. We started out about seven in the morning. By about ten-thirty, he was ready and able to leave the house. I called Billie. They were just leaving church.

She said, "Good. I'll have Harvey at the house. We'll be there before you get there."

"Fine."

I got Lawrence to the car. It was an ordeal. He was so weak. I got him to the car. I was the driver. All these years, he had been the driver. But I became the driver toward the end. I drove him to Harvey's house. They were there, and the doors were open. We went in and sat down on the couch. Lawrence was so proud of his son, and he loved Billie. He had a cup of tea. He sat and chatted. He told them how much he loved them. He looked at Billie, and he said, "I'd give *anything* to see my granddaughter and my great-grandson one more time."

Billie's faster than lightning. She called Amy. Amy came over to the house. It seemed to me like minutes. I couldn't believe it. Lawrence made this request, and within seconds Amy was there with Austin. Austin was just a baby, beautiful, Amy's little son. So Lawrence talked to him and held him. Then he got real tired, and we went home.

That night, Lawrence had to go to bed. He was so tired. Before falling asleep, all he talked about was that beautiful family: his son, Harvey, and Billie, and Amy and Austin. He was a happy man. He was so proud of both of his sons, Harvey and Larry.

As the nurse in an oncology unit, I'm involved in situations where patients are in stage-terminal disease. The thing I hope to achieve as a nurse, and the thing I feel was achieved in Frank's and Lawrence's cases, was to allow the person who's leaving, who's dying, to know their life has been important to you, and how much they meant to you. To remember what they've done, and to know your great love for them.

In Lawrence's and Frank's cases, both of them knew they were loved by their children, by their spouses, and by their friends. That love carries on to today. I'm not a religious person in the manner of going to church, but I have a great belief that there is a hereafter, and I feel like those men are in Heaven together. They're looking down at us. They're proud. As they were proud of us when they were here.

IX. PETS

"Do Not Use This Walk"
Hobo the Alley Cat
Trixie the Hero Dog

"Do Not Use This Walk"

Oftentimes, when people think of Lawrence Detroy, they think in terms of his reputation as a businessman who operated clubs, and a bondsman. But, in reality, Lawrence had a heart that was very big, and he was tenderhearted.

We lived in Winding Falls subdivision, which is off Brownsboro Road, on Ballard's Mill Lane. We had a corner-lot house. The house had a long sidewalk from the mailbox at the street to our front porch. The porch had several columns. Around the front door were windows. Glass windows were set on either side and above the front door.

One day we opened the front door to go out to the mailbox. Above the door we saw pieces of a bird's nest being built. Lawrence said, "Well, look at that! A bird's decided to build a nest!"

I said, "Yeah. I don't know if that's too good of an idea. It's right over our front door."

He took a broom and knocked the beginning of this nest out of the window.

The next day, we went to go to the mailbox, and Lawrence said, "The bird's nest is back."

I said, "You're kidding me!"

He said, "No." He said, "You know, if that bird's that determined to make a nest in that window, I'm giving it the window!"

"Okay, Lawrence, whatever you want to do."

By that evening, the bird had completed its nest right on the ledge above the door. Lawrence went to the garage. I didn't know *what* he was up to. He came out of the garage with a yellow rope and two stakes and a cardboard. He said, "I want you to make a sign for me."

"Okay, Lawrence, whatever."

He took these stakes. He put them on either side of the sidewalk, by the mailbox, all the way out front. He took the yellow rope and he tied it from stake to stake, so it became a barricade to prevent people from walking up our walk. Then he had me put on a sign, "Do Not Use This Walk." That was it.

I said, "Lawrence, what are you doing?"

"Well, if anybody walks up this walk," he said, "they'll disturb the mother bird with the babies. And that's not right. So I'm not going to let them. And I'm not going to tell them why they're not allowed to use the walk. Because if they find out why, they'll come over and bother the bird's nest."

I went, "Oh, ma-a-an." I knew we were in trouble. That subdivision had an association. That association was all-powerful. A resident had to get permission to do *everything*. They had rules for every little, nit-picky thing that you did around your house, much less put a rope across your walk with a sign saying people couldn't use it. I *knew* that we'd get in trouble.

Lawrence called Frank and told him what he was doing. Frank fell out laughing. He said, "Go for it, Fox!"

As the weeks went on, the bird laid eggs. They sat on this nest. Day in and day out, people from the neighborhood would walk past our house. Lawrence and I would use the side door, off the kitchen. That's the side we'd come and go. They would stop us when they'd see us coming and going. They'd say, "Why have you got your sidewalk blocked?"

Lawrence would say, "Suffice it to say it's blocked. I don't want anybody walking on it!"

They'd get excited. "Well, you're not allowed to do that. You can't do that!"

Lawrence said, "Take me to court!" He would not tell these people, and there was a bunch of them, why he had this barrier across his walk.

Finally, the mother bird's eggs hatched. Her babies were little robins. I thought they'd *never* fly. But they finally got big enough to fly, and they flew from the nest. When they did, Lawrence took the broom and brushed down the nest. He went down the walk. He removed the stakes and the rope and the sign. He never told our neighbors what was going on or why, for that six-to-eight-week time period, there was a sign that no one was allowed to use our walk. But that was a typical thing that Lawrence would do that shows his character. He admired the tenacity of this bird, which decided it was going to build a nest, no matter what, in the spot it wanted to build. He liked that.

HOBO THE ALLEY CAT

When Lawrence and I first moved to a condominium on Westport Road, we would pull into the parking lot and park in the back parking area along the creekstone wall. The creekstone wall had landscaping at the top of it. The wall was about four or five feet high. The landscaping was a series of bushes.

When we would pull into our parking spot, several times I thought I saw something move in the bushes. I finally said to Lawrence, "I think there's something living in those bushes there."

He said, "Well, take a look and see."

I got out of the car. I had to stretch to look. Where the water, when it rained, ran down a little hill, it eroded around the root system of a bush. It shaped a cavern. In this cavern was this horrible looking orange cat. His eyes were green. When I looked into this cavern, the cat looked up at me. It just hissed. His teeth were three inches long. It scared me to death. He scared me and I scared him.

I jumped back. I told Lawrence, "My God, it's the meanest, most monstrous cat I've ever seen!" So he went and looked. We both agreed. It was a terrible looking cat.

We went on about our business. Later on I noticed somebody was putting a dish out on this creekstone wall. Obviously to feed this alley cat. A little old lady lived in those condos. I would see her come out carrying this dish. I asked her one day, "Do you feed that cat?"

She said, "Oh yes! That's Hobo."

I said, "Well, what about that cat? How long has it been there? Who does it belong to?"

She said it had been abandoned by somebody over ten years prior to that. For ten years, this cat had lived around this complex. Nobody could touch it. It just survived. It had made a home in this hole by this bush. She felt sorry for it. So she put food out.

I said, "So nobody has ever touched Hobo?"

She said, "To my knowledge, no one can get near that cat. It's just a mean, old alley cat. A tom cat."

When I told Lawrence what she told me, he took that as a challenge.

We were never pet owners. We never had a cat. But Lawrence got the idea that he wanted to cultivate a relationship with this alley cat. He said, "I'll bet I can get that cat to come to our back door."

I'm leery of it. I'm thinking, "I don't know about this killer cat. It's just the meanest-looking thing."

Lawrence started setting a dish of food out for this cat. For a week or two weeks, he set the dish one place. Then he slowly and gradually edged it toward our back porch. Every several weeks, he moved the dish closer and closer to our back porch.

We had a fenced-in patio. There was a gate to the patio. The cat could not get through the closed gate to our back porch. So one morning, Lawrence cut a hole in the bottom of the gate, big enough for the cat to slide through. Of course, the people in the condominium association didn't appreciate a hole being cut in the fence. And, of course, Lawrence said, "I don't know how it got there. It's been there, as far as I know." A few comments were made. Then it was forgotten.

After that, when we would get home, we could hear this cat. The cat would meow to let us know he was in the vicinity. Most of the time we never knew where he was. Then we would go into our front door. We'd prepare some food. Then we would go to the patio door in the back, open the door, and set the food out on the porch. We could see the cat lying on his stomach on the other side of the gate. He peered through this hole, waiting for us to finish our end of the deal.

Then we went back in the door, slid the patio door shut, and closed the shade. Lord help us if we peeked out that shade. The cat would not come out. The cat waited. He finally came inside when he felt nobody was going to touch him. When he felt secure, he would come in and eat his food. Then he would disappear.

This went on for over a year. We developed this relationship with this cat. Nobody ever touched him. One day we came home, and this cat was at our front door. We had never seen this cat at our front door. He was lying down on the steps, right in front of our door. He looked dead. I thought, "Oh, my God, the cat's been killed."

Lawrence thought so, too. He was just lying there. He was a big old cat. When we finally did get him weighed, he weighed almost twenty-eight pounds. He was an enormous, big, old, orange cat. Now he was lying, barely breathing. Blood was everywhere. He had blood all over his face, his throat, and his back. It was matted down, fresh, bright-red blood. He just stared straight ahead. He had really been in a horrible fight. He may have been hit by a car. We suspected a fight because of the way his hair was. A couple of tufts of hair had been pulled out. It was in terrible shape.

Lawrence and I looked at each other. Then we looked at this cat. I thought, "Oh, man, what are we going to do with this cat?" I said, "Lawrence, does this mean we have to touch him?"

"Well, we developed the relationship with him. He's in trouble. He's come to us for help. We're going to have to help him."

I said, "Yeah, but I don't want to touch this cat. There's no telling what kind of varmints are on him. Besides, I don't know if he'll try to bite us."

Lawrence said he wouldn't be able, in the condition he was in, to bite anything. So we went in the house. We got a box. We got some old towels. We carefully wrapped the cat up. The cat did not fight. It was totally flaccid. We picked him up and laid him in the box. I felt like the cat was dying.

We took him across town to a veterinarian we knew. We took him in. We asked the veterinarian what he could do. He said, "My God! What are you doing with this old alley cat?"

Lawrence said, "Don't ask any questions. Just try to help him if you think you can."

"Well, he's been in a horrible fight. He's got teeth marks all over him.

He's got some terrible, open wounds. I don't know. I don't know what we can do for him."

Lawrence said, "Well, it's our fault. We developed a relationship with this cat. We feel responsible. Here's the deal. If you think you can save him, save him. If you can save him, then clean him up and fix him up." We knew he needed to be fixed, because in our condominium area, there were twenty zillion cats that looked like Hobo.

It was against the vet's better thoughts. But he proceeded. He said, "Well, come back tomorrow. We'll see what we can do with the cat."

The next day, the veterinarian called us in the morning. He announced, "You won't believe this animal. I cannot believe how beautiful it is."

This cat had been living in a mudhole for years. It was totally caked with mud. When we went to the vet's to pick this cat up, it was beautiful. It was a bright, beautiful orange, with a snow-white chest. It wasn't solid orange. It sported a snow-white chest, with white under the chin, and white paws. The rest of it was all orange tabby, with shades of real deep orange, and pale orange. His eyes were piercing green. This cat was *beautiful*. It was a pretty cat. Plus, after being fixed, it was docile.

The vet says, "The good news is, we were able to save the cat. He's essentially in good health." They cleaned him up. They got rid of any varmints that were on him. They cleaned him all up. "But," he says, "the bad news is, he's got feline leukemia. So there's two routes you could go. He's in remission, but he's a carrier. If the cat is outside, it will expose other animals to this leukemia."

I said, "Well, what does that mean?"

He said, "That means you're going to have to keep him indoors."

"You mean to tell me we now have a cat, indoors?"

"Yeah."

I said, "This cat hasn't been indoors for ten years."

He said, "Well, he should be a pretty good cat. He should be calm." It was obvious the cat had at some time belonged to someone. "It's up to you. Either he becomes an indoor cat, or maybe we should just put him out. Even though he's in remission, he'll activate eventually in the leukemia. And he's still always a carrier."

Lawrence said, "Well, I don't want to put him out, if he's healthy right now. We'll try it. We'll take him in and see what happens." So we found ourselves being pet owners.

We brought Hobo home. It was as if he had always been there. We got kitty litter for him. We got canned cat food. It was just like he had always been there. There was no adjustment whatsoever. He did not leap on anything. He did not try to damage any furniture. He was so appreciative of having a home. He was just a really wonderful little cat.

Lawrence did not like to have hair on him. So he would sit in his easy chair and take a towel and lay it across his lap. Only then, after he had put the towel across his lap, would Hobo leap up into his lap. He would sit there in Lawrence's lap, as he watched some kind of program. When it was time to go to bed, the cat would leap off his lap. Lawrence would fold up the towel. The cat had a spot in front of the patio door. He never tried to get on our bed, or on our furniture, or on anything. He would just lie at the patio door.

Everything went along very nicely. It was just like we always had this cat. There were no adjustments whatsoever by him to us, or by us to him.

One evening, I had the boys over — my nephews Colin and Liam. They were little. Liam was eleven. Colin was three years younger. They each had a bedroom in our condo. Lawrence and I went to bed. Everybody got along fine. The cat's coming and going, doing his thing, and everybody got along fine.

It was raining when we went to sleep. In the middle of the night, I was awakened by the sound of this cat. The rain had developed into a terrible electric storm. This cat was howling. He was *wailing*. It was wailing as if it had been hurt. I thought, "What is wrong?" Then I heard Hobo run. When a cat as heavy as this runs, it sounds like a herd of elephants. He came galloping in. He leaped up on the bed. He ran as hard as he could up to where my head was. He began shoving me with his paws. The whole time he's wailing. I thought, "What is wrong with this animal? This animal has flipped out." I shoved him off the bed. I thought, "God, I can't understand what is his problem."

Then I heard him run around the bed. It was a king-size bed. He ran to the foot of the bed, across the foot, and then back up on the other side.

He leaped up on the bed and did the same thing to Lawrence. Lawrence jumped up. He went, "God, what is wrong with this cat?" He shoved the cat off the bed. He said, "Beverly, what's happened to Hobo?"

"I don't know what's wrong with him. The cat's flipped out."

We tried to go back to sleep. We shoved the cat off the bed.

I heard him run into the boys' rooms. He leaped up on Liam's bed. Liam jumped up in bed, and I heard him holler out, "What's going on? Get off, Hobo!" He shoved Hobo off the bed.

Hobo ran into little Colin's room. He did the same thing to Colin. We heard Colin wake up. The cat had managed to awaken Liam, Colin, myself and Lawrence.

I thought, "I cannot believe this. What is wrong with this animal?"

Then he came galloping back into our room again. It's three or four in the morning. I barely opened my eyes. I'm facing the wall of my bedroom, and the curtains to our patio door were open. Because Lawrence loved to watch and listen to the rain, and it had been raining that night, we had left the curtains open. I opened my eyes and looked at the antique white wall of our bedroom, but the wall was no longer antique white. It was *pink*. I thought, "What?" And I looked again. "That wall is pink. Why is it pink?"

Meanwhile, the cat leaped up on the bed doing everything it could. It was attacking me. The whole time it never stopped wailing. Just hollering, like, "Please, listen to me! Listen to me!" So I sat up in the bed. I looked out our patio door at another set of condos a hundred yards away. They're all town homes.

When I looked through the patio door at the condos that were far away, I saw flames shooting up from the roof of the condos. The flames shot as high as twenty to thirty feet up in the air. The whole cluster of four condos was on fire. It was all at the top part of the condo. It was all coming from the roof.

We contacted the fire department. The fire department came out. They had a hell of a time containing this fire. The people all got out of the condos. We watched those poor people in their pajamas trying to save their worldly belongings. We watched them drag out couches and chairs. They piled clothes and possessions out in the courtyard of the condo. The firemen parked in the parking lot as close as possible to the building. Their hoses were shooting water over one set of condos to get to the set that was on fire. They fought from two different angles to contain this fire. Finally they put the fire out. But the cluster of condos was burnt to the ground. Nothing was left.

They determined that during the storm, lightning had struck the roof of one of these condos, and it had caused an electric fire which had smoldered and finally shot up in flames. The residents had not been aware of it because it burned from the roof down. Lawrence and I and Colin and Liam stood on our porch and patio watching the scene of this fire. We stopped and looked down at this cat, Hobo, who was sitting there as if to say, "I thought you people would *never* get up!" He was just as calm as could be. From that moment on, "Hobo the Alley Cat" became "Hobo the Hero Alley Cat."

Hobo lived maybe two years longer after that. One day I came home, and he didn't look right. The vet had told us that when the leukemia finally activated, the cat could suffer a lot, or he could go quickly. I knew instantly something was wrong with Hobo. We took him to the vet. That night, Hobo just laid his head down and died.

This animal was a wonderful, wonderful cat. He lived, essentially, a marvelous last few years of his life. He had survived and lived out in the wild for ten years. He had been abandoned and had learned to live in the wild, without letting anybody touch him. There is no way to know all he endured and experienced during that time. And then during the last few years of his life he became a house pet. He had a home. He was well-fed and taken care of. He was very well-loved. He gave much more, probably, than we were able to give to him. But he was a wonderful pet. He's probably in heaven.

TRIXIE THE HERO DOG

Lawrence's half-brother, Jerry Gogan, had a personality that was hard for a lot of people to take. He was gravelly and gruff and rude. He was firm and set in his ways. But essentially I liked the guy. I liked him. One thing you could say about Jerry Gogan — he was never phony. All his life, Jerry loved animals. All his life, Jerry Gogan had some little dog tagging along behind him.

On her deathbed, Lawrence's mother's biggest worry was that the family would abandon Jerry. Jerry was an alcoholic. And even though he had stopped drinking some twenty years earlier, he had literally destroyed his health. He was not able to take care of himself. He had to walk with a cane. He couldn't walk very far. He was short of breath. He was a smoker all his life. He never gave up his cigarettes. With all his physical problems, he simply was not able to take care of himself.

Lawrence's mother knew the one person who would keep his word was Lawrence. She requested him to please allow Jerry to live in her home until the day he died, which is exactly what Lawrence did. Lawrence never missed a beat. He took care of his brother the rest of his life.

Jerry had this one little dog. The dog's name was Trixie. It looked exactly like the little Benji dog that's so popular. Trixie was a "Heinz 57" dog, a little, slight dog. But it was just full of energy. This little dog, with its hair hanging down in its eyes, was always wiggling and happy. It just adored Jerry. This gravelly old man and Trixie were a pair.

Every day, they had a set routine. Jerry got up at a certain time in the morning. He went and got his newspaper. He took Trixie for a walk. He fixed them both breakfast. They followed this little routine, day in and day out.

Lawrence's responsibility was to go get Jerry's grocery orders. But the biggest responsibility was to make sure that Trixie ate. When we brought Jerry's grocery to his house, the first concern was not what Jerry ate, but what Trixie ate. These two really loved each other.

Jerry began to have a lot of difficulty breathing. He progressively deteriorated in his health. He hated going to doctors. We had to force him to go to a doctor. One day, we went by to see him, and he looked markedly worse. His color was ashen. He was very strained. Lawrence tried to talk him into going to the hospital. He absolutely refused. He had this old, gravelly voice. "I ain't going to that old, damn hospital!" He was really, really firm about it.

Lawrence thought, "Well, I'll let him go one night and think it over." The next morning we would take him to the doctor or the hospital. So the following morning, we got over to the house early. It was a little house on Barrett Avenue. It had windows all around it. All of the curtains were drawn.

As we pulled up, Lawrence said, "Jerry's dead." Part of Jerry's routine in the morning was to open all the curtains in the house.

And as we got out of the car, we could hear this incessant barking. Just barking, barking, barking, barking. We looked at the curtains. Trixie was straining. This little dog was straining to reach up to this window. You could see her leaping, and barking and barking and barking and barking.

We unlocked the door and went in. The house was dark. We found Jerry in bed. He had died in his sleep.

This little dog was running circles around the bed. It kept barking and barking and carrying on. We got the coroner. We took care of everything regarding Jerry. But we ended up with this dog. We brought Trixie home with us. Trixie was just pitiful. Trixie laid her head down by the kitchen door and would not move. She just lay there.

We talked to our veterinarian friend. The vet said, "The dog's not going to live unless something can inspire it to eat and drink." Trixie refused to eat. She refused to drink. She didn't make a sound. She just lay there. It was sad to see — this poor little dog mourning for her master.

Jerry had that gravelly voice. He was real. Someone who didn't know him might think he was mad at them. But that was just Jerry's way. After a couple of days of Trixie refusing to eat, we were beside ourselves trying to figure out how to inspire this dog to snap out of it.

Lawrence came in the kitchen door one day. He looked down. He said, in a voice that was similar to Jerry's, "Trixie!" Trixie's ears popped up. She just looked. He said, "Come here, Trixie!" just the way Jerry would have. Trixie jumped up and ran over to Lawrence. From that moment on, she snapped out of it, and was able to adapt to living with us.

Trixie was a good little dog and we loved her dearly. But we had just bought the Golden Fox, and we were sacrificing long, long hours to this restaurant and bar. It wasn't fair to the dog. So we found a couple, Sam and Donna, who had two children, a little toddler and another little girl. They absolutely loved dogs, and they were looking for a pet for their little toddler. We tested them out to see if Trixie would adapt to them. Trixie loved them instantly. She just fell in love with this couple and their kids. She loved this little toddler. So we gave Trixie to this couple.

This couple lived in Indiana in a small neighborhood. They had a fenced-in backyard. The little toddler would go out back and play with all her toys. Trixie would go out and sit with this baby. The dog was the little girl's bodyguard. She just loved this toddler. And the toddler could do anything to Trixie — pull her ears, pull her hair, pull her tail, push her, play with her — and Trixie always loved it. They got along famously.

The next-door neighbors had taken a dog that had been a guard dog, and decided they were going to make this dog a pet. This was a police dog, a German shepherd. This dog was so mean and so vicious that they had it chained to a tree in the backyard. They were scared to feed the dog. The dog was just snarling. It was a vicious, vicious dog. They should never even have tried to keep the dog, but they felt sorry for it. They thought they could make it into a house pet.

This dog was in one yard. Trixie was in the other yard. There was a chain-link fence in between. Every day, when Trixie would go out in the back with this little girl, this dog would snarl and pull on the chain and bark. It lashed out like it wanted to get to the toddler or to Trixie. This worried Sam and Donna. They spoke to the neighbors about it. The neighbors said, "Don't worry about it. The chain's real strong. The dog's not going to get loose." Even the neighbors were aware they could never tame this dog.

One afternoon, the little girl went out in the backyard and was sitting and playing in her usual spot. Trixie was lying down beside her taking a nap. The German shepherd dog managed to break its chain. It then proceeded to leap over the fence. When it leaped over the fence, it lunged at this little girl. This little girl was just a baby. She was not even three. She looked up and here was this dog lunging at her. Trixie immediately woke up and flew to the dog and grabbed it. There was a terrific amount of noise.

Donna said she happened to look out the window at that moment. She said, "I was horrified." The German shepherd was leaping at her little girl. Then Trixie was leaping at the German shepherd, in between the little girl and the shepherd. Trixie grabbed the German shepherd by the neck. The German shepherd and Trixie were locked in a horrible dogfight. Donna ran out back. She screamed for Sam. Sam went and got a gun, a pistol. He went running out the back door. They grabbed up the little girl. They could not separate the dogs. The dogs were rolling. Trixie was no match for the German shepherd. The shepherd just totally tore the little dog to shreds. Sam took his gun and shot the German shepherd between the eyes.

He told Lawrence and me about this. He was a Southern boy and had a long drawl when he talked. He said, "Weeell, I shot the dog between the eyes. I picked the son of a bitch up by the collar. I carried it over to the fence. The neighbors were out there, looking. I picked the dog up, threw it over the fence, and said, 'Here's your dog back. Could've killed my kid.'"

There was never, ever a word said between the neighbors and Sam. Sam's standing there with the gun in his hand. He could easily have killed the people, too. He was so upset over the fact of losing his little dog and almost losing his daughter.

Trixie, the little "Heinz 57" mutt, died protecting her master.

X. GOOD-BYES

Letting Go
Saying Good-byes
The Notes

LETTING GO

Lawrence was essentially a healthy man. He had bouts of physical problems. But he was always able to take care of himself and rebound from the different types of surgeries and difficulties he had. He never was really a sick man, per se. He had the will and ability to keep on going.

But in the last five years of our marriage, there was a marked decrease in Lawrence's health. He was becoming short of breath and weaker. His stamina was not like it was. But he still had his strong will. He still maintained his wit and ability to keep going.

Lawrence and Frank Haddad had a unique relationship. They loved one another like brothers. They spoke every night on the telephone. Either Frank would call Lawrence, or Lawrence would call Frank. They would banter about the day's issues, politics, and whatever was happening. They both would banter about these things.

I heard the conversation from Lawrence's end, and JoAnn heard it from Frank's end. Every night when Frank would call or Lawrence would call him, the first thing Lawrence would say was, "Well, how's JoAnn?" Lawrence just loved JoAnn. JoAnn was closer than a friend, more like a sister to Lawrence. Frank and I would laugh, because we understood they were like two peas in a pod in their personalities.

They were *so* loyal to each other. Lawrence would say, "I'll hold the lantern and you dig the grave, JoAnn." The two of them had a great relationship.

But I could hear every night, Lawrence would ask Frank, "How's JoAnn?"

Frank would say, "JoAnn's on the couch," and she had her shoes off, or she had her feet propped up, or whatever. It was a continual thing. After Lawrence found out JoAnn was doing okay, then they could carry on their conversation.

When it became apparent Lawrence's health was failing, Frank didn't want his friend to be sick. He was very defensive of Lawrence. It upset him terribly to see his friend decline. We watched the shadow of the man walk down the lane. We saw him lose weight and become weaker and weaker.

Frank became upset over the situation. Always before we were able to pull a rabbit out of the hat in regard to Lawrence's health. We were able to find some fix to fix him. A surgery, or a medicine, or something. There was always something we could do to help. The doctors told us his lungs were failing him. There truly was nothing more we could do. We could only try to maintain the situation the best we could at home.

Lawrence was very, very adamant that he did not want to be hospitalized any more than necessary. He did not like people to hover about him when he was ill.

Toward the end, especially in the last year, he had many bouts with illnesses. But only one other person knew he was sick, and that was Frank Haddad. This was per Lawrence's request. He did not want his sons to know how ill he was. He did not want anybody to know. That was his request. His personal desire was for people to see him in the shape he wanted them to see, not weak.

The problem was that, in his youth, Lawrence had had tuberculosis. In those days, there was no treatment for TB except for pneumothoraxes. That was a procedure in which a doctor would take a needle and collapse your lung and give your lungs time to heal the lesions. Then they would do these procedures repeatedly, hoping to heal all the lesions on your lungs so that you could survive. Most people died of TB. But Lawrence didn't.

Every time they did a pneumothorax treatment, it caused a certain amount of scarring in his lungs. As time went on, with repeated treatments, the scarring got thicker and thicker in his lungs. Toward the end, he had

214

only a thirty-percent lung capacity. This was truly the part that was ending his life. There was nothing you could do for this particular condition.

Frank got upset. He felt we weren't doing enough for Lawrence. He would call me every day and make suggestions on things to do to help Lawrence. Let's send him to the Mayo Clinic. Let's send him to this doctor. Let's send him to that doctor. Why can't we do this? I've read this article. He was adamant to try to do something to stop the deterioration in Lawrence's condition.

It got to the point where I began to feel that Frank was badgering me. He would call in the morning and want to know where Lawrence was, and I would tell him. Then he would say that was too much on him. Then he'd call me in the afternoon and say, "Well did he come home to lay down?"

I'd say, "No, he had lunch with So-and-So." It became a battle between Frank Haddad and me over Lawrence's health. It was so upsetting to think Frank felt there were things that could be done that we weren't doing. That wasn't the case at all.

Finally I decided Frank and I really, really had to talk about the condition of his friend. I called Frank on the phone at his office and asked him to set aside some time and clear his desk, and let me come down and talk to him, which I had never done before. I said I wanted to have this meeting just between him and me. Neither Lawrence nor JoAnn would be there. Just us two. Frank agreed.

I went downtown. It was very difficult for me to do this. When I got to the office, Rose was at the desk. She was a wonderful, wonderful woman who served as receptionist for Frank. She said, "Mr. Haddad's waiting on you."

I said, "Fine."

When I went in the office, Frank did have his desk cleared. He was waiting patiently for me. He really didn't know what I wanted to discuss with him.

I talked to him about Lawrence. I explained to him what the doctors had told me about Lawrence's condition. There truly was nothing we could do for Lawrence to stop the inevitable progress of the disease. I asked Frank, "How would you feel if I told you to sit in the chair?"

He said, "Well, I wouldn't like that, Beverly."

I said, "Well, what you're asking me to do is to tell Lawrence to sit." Frankly, if I had asked Lawrence to do that, he would have done it. He loved me. If I would have demanded Lawrence to just sit, that's exactly what he would've done. He trusted me. He knew I would do things in his best interest.

But telling this man to not leave the house, demanding him to just rest, and to stay in bed and become a patient, essentially, was the same as sending him to a nursing home. I couldn't do that to Lawrence. I told Frank this. I said, "Frank, I cannot stop time. I cannot give Lawrence his youth. I can't give him his lungs. I wish I could, but I can't."

I repeated to Frank that asking Lawrence to sit would be equivalent to putting him in a nursing home. I couldn't do that. I would love to do anything I could to help Lawrence. But the one thing I would never do was take away his dignity. If I put limits on him and told him, "Don't go here," and "Don't do this," and "Don't do that," and put limits on him, that would destroy the man as we knew him.

Frank listened to me. He understood what I was saying. That day, Frank was so sad. He was sitting on the edge of that big, enormous chair in his office, leaning forward on the desk. As we talked and I discussed what the doctors had told me about Lawrence's condition, he fell back in his chair and hung his head. He said, "I just don't want to lose my friend."

I said, "I don't either, Frank."

We both loved Lawrence. And that day we came to an agreement that, as a team, we would do everything we could to make Lawrence's last days good ones. We would try our best, without Lawrence being aware of it, to protect him. Lawrence would never complain or say he wasn't feeling well. We agreed that, when I knew Lawrence was going some place, I would let Frank know. Then we would have people staked out who could give us a call, and say, "Lawrence doesn't look too good," or whatever. One way or another, we could get to him and try to help him.

Together we came to an agreement. It was a hard one for both of us. It meant letting Lawrence go. But we had to let him go in his own way.

Lawrence would take me to work and pick me up. Lawrence loved to drive me places. Frankly, I liked it. We would take the time when we drove places to talk. He would tell many, many stories. We would go through a community or a neighborhood, and something would remind him of a story. He told me the stories. I loved that. I always loved it, even if I had heard the stories a hundred times before. I thoroughly enjoyed that. The stories would always be funny and exciting.

But one day, I knew the end was very near with Lawrence. I worked from seven at night until seven in the morning at the hospital. Lawrence would pick me up in the morning. He would pull out in front of Baptist Hospital. When he'd see me walk through the door, he would always open the driver's door, get out, then open the door for me to get into the car. This was Lawrence's style. He always liked to open doors for me, and I always appreciated it. I thought that was a natural thing that he did. This was the gentleman in Lawrence. He loved to do those things for us.

It used to aggravate JoAnn and I, because when the four of us would go someplace, Frank would bolt out the door to go wherever we were going. JoAnn and I sat in the car and waited for Lawrence to get out, go around to the side of the car, open her door to let her out, then open my door to let me out. Sometimes we would be sitting in the car and we'd be grumbling, "For Christ's sake, when is he going to get to this side of the car?" But this was what Lawrence wanted to do, and we loved it.

But this particular morning, I came out of the hospital. Lawrence was sitting in the usual place. But there was something different about him. I could see from a distance that he didn't look right. As I got closer to the car, he didn't even know I was there. I got all the way up to the car and tapped on the window. He was just sitting there, very ashen and white-faced. He stared straight ahead, as if in shock. I tapped on the window several times. Finally he snapped out of it, and he looked at me. I asked him to unlock the door.

He flipped the lock on the handle of the door. I got in the automobile. I said, "What's wrong?"

He said, "I almost died last night."

I said, "What do you mean?"

He told me he had gotten ill through the night. He thought it was something he had eaten during the day prior to that, perhaps food poisoning. He had gotten ill, and he had stayed ill all night long, with dysentery. He had tremors. He was chilling. He said, "I couldn't breathe."

I was very upset. He hadn't called me or let me know. I had no idea this was going on. I had spoken to him before he went to bed that night. I always called him from the hospital. He sounded fine.

But he was very ill. I was afraid he wasn't able to drive the automobile. I asked him, "Do you want me to drive the car?" First off, I wanted him to go to the emergency room, but he refused.

He said, "I think I'll be okay if we can just get home."

So I said, "Alright." Lawrence was very determined. Once he made up his mind about something, no one could break it. There was no sense arguing with him about going to the emergency room.

I asked him if he wanted me to drive the automobile. He said, "No. If you drive, I don't think we could make it." He said, "I need to have something to do. Let me drive the automobile."

I said, "Alright."

On the trip home, we're riding down the road. The car is swerving from side to side. He's driving ever so slow. I thought, "Oh my God, we're never going to get there!" I'm telling him, "Get in the lane. Move over to the right. Move over to the left." I'm trying to guide him. He's doing okay. But it was a struggle for him to get us from Baptist Hospital to our home.

What normally would take twenty minutes, took forty minutes. But through the entire trip, he kept trying to talk and trying to tell me about what happened to him the night before. He made plans on what we could do to help him once we got home.

We got to the house. He stopped the car. He was not able even to open his door. I got out of the car, went around to his side, and opened the door. This man who was always so strong, even in illness, was so weak he couldn't get out of the automobile. I had to literally pull him out of the car. I had to stand him up. He was so wobbly. He put his arms around my shoulders, and I helped him to the house. It seemed like we never were going to make it to that door, but we did.

Several times we had to stop to give him time to rest. But we finally got into the house. I called the doctor and explained to him what had happened. We worked out a game plan on how to help Lawrence during the day. All day long I kept giving him medications to try to clear out his system of this food poisoning. Every time he would become sick and have dysentery, I would force him to drink fluids and Gatorade. I was trying to keep his electrolytes up. He would become deathly ill. Then he would go to bed.

The only person who knew of this condition was Frank. I had talked to Frank that morning. I had to keep Frank posted on what was going on. I also talked to the doctor several times during the day about how he was progressing.

After a long morning and afternoon, about nine o'clock that evening, finally Lawrence improved. He began to feel better. He said, "Let's just go to bed." So we went to bed.

I remember this as being probably one of the tenderest moments in our entire marriage. I think many couples probably go through this when they have to deal with illnesses. When we finally lay down in the bed, it came over me. I knew he would not be with us much longer. He never liked to see me cry. I tried not to ever do that in his company. But I remember lying down in the bed, and the tears just started. They started flowing. I didn't sob out loud. I just cried. He knew that I was crying. He sensed it, like I did.

He reached over and took my hand and kissed it. He held my hand to his chest, and squeezed my hand. I couldn't talk. I couldn't say anything. He didn't say anything, either. But for that entire night he held my hand and squeezed it.

I don't remember falling asleep, but I finally did. And in the morning when I awakened, he still held my hand. He was still squeezing it in his sleep. That morning, he said, "I think it's time I go to the hospital," and he did. He died two days later.

That night was one of the most tender nights I ever had with Lawrence.

Saying Good-byes

The singular characteristic Lawrence Detroy and Frank Haddad shared is that they both did everything they wanted to do. Both of these men managed to do pretty much whatever they wanted to do. They always enjoyed themselves. It didn't matter how much heat was on them, or how bad a situation might be. They would manage to see the humor in it and the excitement in it. And later on, they'd describe whatever happened in stories that would fascinate other people.

The two guys had the same type of wit about life, period. They could see qualities in people that nobody else could see. There might be a person everybody else thought was a loser or useless, but both Lawrence and Frank would see some little thread of goodness in this person and befriend them. Then these individuals would be intensely loyal to Lawrence and Frank. At both Frank's and Lawrence's funerals, there was an incredibly diverse variety of people. These guys were legendary for the little things they did for so many other individuals. It was their nature. It showed their character.

Lawrence and Frank grew up in a similar era. They lived separate lives. But they were similar in their outlook that nobody was ever too big or too little for them.

The poem written for Lawrence by a little, alcoholic guy at the funeral was beautiful. It was amazing to think this little guy, Jimmy Wilson, could sit and write this poem. This little guy was an abused person. He was lonely. Lawrence befriended him. He came up to me at the funeral home. It was so sad because Lawrence was like a father to him that he never had.

Jimmy had a terrible childhood. He was so very sad. He stuttered a little bit. He said, "I-I-I'm so sorry about the F-F-Fox. I-I-I'm s-so sorry." Jimmy was an alcoholic. I was concerned about his alcoholism and worried he would just totally go off. The previous year, Jimmy had started sending Lawrence and me letters. He had never done this in all the years before.

I asked Lawrence, "What are these letters?"

He said, "I don't know. I haven't opened them. Something from Jimmy. I don't know what they are." He thought they were clippings.

I opened them, and in these letters was poetry. Lawrence did not read poetry. He said, "Well, what's he doing that for? What's he sending me poetry for?"

I said, "Because, in his mind, he's putting something down on paper he's feeling. That's his way of expressing himself."

Jimmy had all these poems notarized before he sent them to us. So it was an honor that he would give us these poems. A lot of these poems were nonsensical or poorly written, but a few occasionally came out quite lovely. I was surprised about that.

At the funeral home, I asked Jimmy if he would write me something for Lawrence. I figured that might keep him from getting drunk.

The next day he turned up at the funeral home. He had a piece of long, yellow legal paper. It was all folded up. He came to me and said, "I-I-I did this for you. It's probably not any good. But I did this for you. It's for the Fox."

And so I took it, and I looked at it. I was amazed. It was a very nice poem. It was a really good description of Lawrence. I gave it to Frank. He said, "Did he write that?"

I said, "Yeah."

He said, "Well, that's amazing." Frank and I determined that we were going to have it read at Lawrence's funeral.

"Jimmy," I said. "Jimmy, you're going to be there tomorrow, aren't you?"

"I can't, Mrs. Detroy. I-I-I don't have a coat."

"You don't have a coat?"

"No."

"Oh," I said. "So you're saying Mr. Detroy was a hypocrite?"

"Well, what do you mean by that?" he said. "He wasn't a hypocrite."

"Well, then you're saying you're not coming to the funeral because Lawrence was a snob and he would want you to wear a coat." I badgered him. "All you have to do is wash your face and comb your hair and be there, Jimmy. Lawrence was your friend. And I want you to be there." I didn't want to tell him I was going to have his poem read out loud. If I told him that, then he would for sure go get drunk.

Jimmy showed the next day. He had on a navy-blue gabardine windbreaker jacket. He looked nice. He looked clean and nice. He was shy. When we walked in the church, I stopped at his pew. I said, "Jimmy, may I have your permission to read your poem?"

He was dumbfounded. "Well, y-y-yes, Mrs. Detroy. It's for you."

I said, "Okay." I had my little niece read that poem. I thought it epitomized Lawrence. Lawrence had seen goodness in this little guy where very few people, if any, had found any value at all. And yet, he did end up writing a beautiful little poem. A lot of people commented about that. I thought that showed how they could see special things in people that nobody else could see. Lawrence never did appreciate poetry, but he'd have appreciated this poem.

The night the hospital called me and told me Lawrence was dying, I called Frank. We'd thought we had him stable. I called Frank. His voice on the phone wailed. He went, "Oh, no! Not Lawrence!"

I told him I'd call him from the hospital when I got there. Harvey and Billie came and got me. I couldn't drive. He was so very sad. He'd already died by the time I got to the hospital. I called Frank and told him.

I stood by the bed. Lawrence lay in the bed. He was dead. I had the phone in my ear. Frank talked to me for I don't know how long. It probably was ten or fifteen minutes. It seemed like a long time. He was going on and on about his friend.

THE NOTES

I'm never in JoAnn Haddad's company that I don't look at her and remember how much her husband loved her. I think sometimes JoAnn knows this. At other times I'm not sure she's aware.

Frank absolutely worshipped JoAnn. They had such a beautiful relationship and marriage. That's not to say everything was perfect all the time, but they were perfect for one another. JoAnn was patient with Frank, and loyal. And Frank was patient and loyal with JoAnn. Frank was such a funny man. He knew how to push buttons with JoAnn.

We pushed Frank's buttons, but Frank was also a needler. He would plot all day long for something to get a rise out of JoAnn. On the surface, his deep love for his wife may not have been obvious. But seeing Frank, and being in his company, we understood he loved his wife so much.

JoAnn worried about Frank. She worried about his weight. She worried about him working too hard. She worried about the stress of the high-profile cases he handled. She tried her best to tone him down. But she could only do so much. Frank was happy at what he was doing, and he did it his way. That song Sinatra has, "I Did It My Way," describes exactly Frank *and* Lawrence. Both of them lived their lives in their own way. Nobody else could tell them what to do or how to do something. They were never afraid to make a decision. Lawrence used to say, "If you've never made a mistake, then you've never made a decision." Both those men made mistakes. And they did things other people probably didn't agree with. But they were true to themselves.

JoAnn did everything she could to help maintain Frank's diet. Frank was always losing weight. I'd say, "Frank, how are you doing?"

He'd say, "Oh, I'm doing fine."

I'd say, "How are you doing on your diet?"

"Oh, I lost five pounds."

I never could quite get it down. Was this was the same five pounds he lost every time? Or was this a new five pounds? It was always five pounds.

JoAnn was conscientious about trying to fix him food. She encouraged him to try to cut down on fats. She'd send food with him to the office. She hoped that would be all he would eat. Frank would eat whatever was in the brown paper bag, along with going to lunch. That was what Frank would do. JoAnn didn't stand a chance of keeping him on a diet.

She would frequently write a little note and put it in with the food she sent for Frank. I don't know what the notes said. They were just little notes to Frank from her. She never really thought much about it. She just did that. JoAnn's a very sweet woman who loved her husband a lot. She wanted him to know that.

When Frank died, his associates found all of these notes in his desk in a box. He'd kept them and collected them over the years. When I think about that, it makes my heart fill up. This man was so busy. He had such tremendous stresses in his life and so many cases he was handling. Business ventures and big events were always happening all around him. Still, he took the time to read these little notes that his wife sent him. He put them in a special place in his desk. That summarizes how Frank felt about his wife, how much he loved JoAnn.

End